Fit & Swarm 34 Defense Playbook

ISBN: 978-1-7351591-4-0

Introduction

Introduction

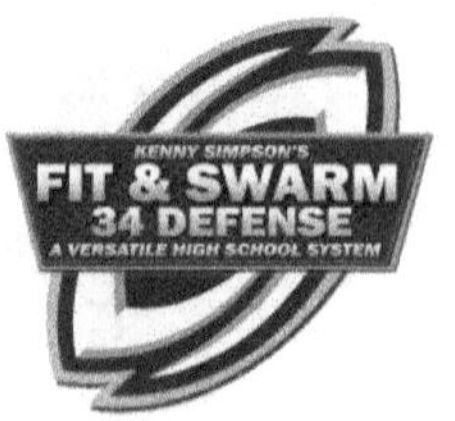

A long time ago a very young 25-year-old version of me became a defensive coordinator in Montgomery, Alabama. I was blessed to work at a 4A school with some great young men and great coaches. Like any younger coach, I ran what I had been taught. So, we were a 4-4 cover 3 team.

Much has changed since then. I became a head football coach at the same school and hired a great defensive coordinator that installed the 3-3 stack defense. I then moved states to Arkansas in 2011 as a head football coach, and we continued to run the 3-3.

After a few rough years, we needed to revamp our defense and moved to the 3-4. It was one of the best things I have seen for us on defense. The versatility is needed in today's game and the simplicity it offers helps us to install it quickly. If we have a more experienced team, we can install more, and if we are playing with a younger group, we can still create the illusion of a complex defense with a few simple calls.

Introduction

I hope you gain something from this book. My goal is to share our system for those looking to work on the defensive side of the ball. There are many great defenses to study, but this one is geared for a high school program.

As the name implies it is the "Fit and Swarm" defense. At many of my stops we have not always had the fastest athletes, so we have had to focus on exactly where we are to take our aiming points. Once our athletes understand that, we expect them to SWARM to the ball as a unit.

This book is meant to simply be an introduction to give you the "bones" of the defense. Each year we add what our athletes are capable of doing into the playbook. My hope is coaches can take this and either install the system or at least gain a useful piece to add into their defense.

Feel free to reach out if you have any questions:

@Fbcoachsimpson
FBCoachSimpson@gmail.com
FBCoachSimpson.com

The entire system can be found here:
(Use your camera on your phone to open link.)

Recommendations

Quotes

"Great overview of the 3-4 defense. Coach Simpson does a great job breaking down his 3-4 defense."
– Mike Weaver

"Coach Simpson does a great job of explaining all of the details that must be considered when assembling a blitz package."
- Jeff Weiland

" I worked with Coach Simpson for nine seasons. I learned most of what I know about running the 34 system from him. He does an excellent job teaching schemes and concepts while simplifying as much as possible for the kids!"
- Brian Reardon

Quotes

"I love Kenny Simpson's 3-4 Fit & Swarm defense because he keeps it simple. Eliminate all the unnecessary checks, a few blitzes, and a couple coverages. Let the kids play fast. Coach Simpson's defense does that and this book is laid in very easy to read and even more importantly, easy to understand format and language. I highly recommend."

- Rick Stewart

FIND
WAY

KENNY SIMPSON'S
FIT & SWARM
34 DEFENSE
A VERSATILE HIGH SCHOOL SYSTEM

FIND WAY
Table of Contents
KENNY SIMPSON'S
FIT & SWARM
34 DEFENSE
A VERSATILE HIGH SCHOOL SYSTEM

FIND
WAY

KENNY SIMPSON'S
FIT & SWARM
34 DEFENSE
A VERSATILE HIGH SCHOOL SYSTEM

Defensive Theory

Each defensive system will have a general theory behind it. There are many types of 3-4 defenses that a coach can decide to implement. Here are the keys we teach our players DAY 1 and our core beliefs:

1) **No big plays on busts** – We define a big play that we gave up as a 20-yard pass that the player was uncovered or was not touched. Or a 20-yard run that the ball carrier was never touched or broke an unblocked defender's tackle. In football today, big plays tend to happen, but we want our players to understand that we want the offense to have to earn everything they get. We do not panic on first downs, but do not allow big plays.

2) **Play the situations** – We want our players to understand that the game will be won on 3rd/4th down plays, red-zone percentage, and when we have the offense backed up in their own area of the field. Many times, simply making sure our players are aware of what is happening in the game will allow us to be successful.

3) **Players Over Plays** – Stop their best players. As simple as that sounds, many times as coaches we are so consumed by the scheme, we forget that it needs to be designed to stop the other team's best players. We want the flexibility to take the other team's best players out of the equation by getting our numbers right in all sets at all times.

4) **Be aggressive at the right time** – Understanding when and where to look for turnovers is key. We love causing turnovers, but we want to always work this inside the game plan. Knowing the situation and tendencies of the opposition gives us a chance to be aggressive at the right time.

5) **Know your responsibility each play** – We never want to be beat before the ball is snapped. It is key we keep our game plan as simple as needed for our players to always know their responsibility. This defense can be as simple or complex as the players can handle. But we will never become so complex our players are not sure of their job pre-snap.

6) **9-10 Hats to the Ball** – SWARM. Effort must be a given. The only players not swarming are responsible for cutback/RPO game. This needs to become the culture of the defense.

7) **Big hits are fun, but sure tackling wins** – We will spend most of our individual time working on angles and tackling form. This part of the game will determine the difference in a great play and "almost" a great play. Must be sure tacklers.

Why the 34

There are plenty of options to choose from in a defense; this is why I believe the 34 gives our athletes a chance to be successful in today's game.

1) **It allows more athletes on the field** – Pretty simple, we are taking off a defensive lineman and replacing him with a faster more athletic player.

2) **Much more flexibility** – We believe we can jump into a 4 front or a 5 front with just a few calls. If we start in a 4 front, moving to a 3 front is much more challenging.

3) **Matches up against the Spread** – Today's football is much more shotgun and spread personnel groupings, and this defense adjusts more quickly to match whatever the other team throws out each week.

4) **Able to move the front and stunt every play** – It is much easier to stunt and be willing to bring 2nd level players in a 3 front than in a 4 front with much less risk involved.

5) **Easier to disguise coverage** – Starting each play in a 2-high balanced look allows us to roll coverage or even match up without as many pre-snap give-a-ways as a 4 front would.

6) **Easier to "take away players" from the offense** – By simply rolling down a safety post snap, or widening an OLB we can now add numbers to take away a gifted WR. For a run heavy team, we can roll a safety into the box.

Personnel Choices

Getting the right players on the field is as important as the scheme. When building a 34 defense, this is how I would pick athletes:

Safeties are the hardest to find
We always start with the safety position when picking personnel and try to develop as many as possible in lower grades. This player must be your best defensive player. He must tackle well, cover and communicate. They also must have a good football IQ and feel for space.

This position is usually going to have 80-120 tackles and have the chance to force 8-10 turnovers a season. It is the most important spot on the defense.

-If you find players that almost fit this mold, we usually move them to other positions. In a perfect world the OLB and Safeties would look very similar. Generally, for us we take our younger player, or maybe not as football "savy" player and move him down to OLB. We take the athletic ones that won't quite tackle well enough for safety and move to corner.

Our "Dog" will have over 100 tackles almost each season as we work to get him involved in the run game as often as possible. Usually, he is your best football player on the defensive side of the ball.

Our "Free" is often the better athlete of the two as he will be in coverage more often and making plays in space. Both must be willing to tackle, but this player often makes plays that save touchdowns.

Personnel Choices

Outside Backers are usually the best athletes
While we would love to play our best athletes at safety, often those players may not be as comfortable in coverage or not a great communicator so this is where they would end up. We want athletes at these spots. This position must set an edge in your defense and must be able to cover.

We will usually pick better athletes and not be as concerned about size at this position. We do not often see teams that would force them to play in a 9-technique and if we do, we have a few tricks to help him if he is an undersized player.

Usually our "End" is the larger of the two and will be involved more in the running game in the box. Our "Will" is often a 5th DB and handles all trips concepts.

Inside Linebackers come in all shapes/speeds and sizes
While these two need to be great at tackling and it would be great if they were athletic also, that is not a requirement for both. We generally ask our "Sam" to be of a 4th defensive lineman as far as his fits and he usually in the box most of the time. He does need to be thick enough or tough enough to take on lead blocks.

Our "Mike" is usually the more athletic of the two linebackers as he will be asked to cover more ground and cover more in the passing game. One of these two needs to be able to call your front and stunts.

Cornerback play
While we would prefer that we have players that are great athletes at these positions, that is not always the reality of the situation. We do attempt to put our best athletes at this position, and we will adjust our coverages based on what this player is able to do.

We teach "pattern" read so this player needs to have at least a basic football "IQ" in him as we want to switch routes and need to be able to read as we move.

Defensive Linemen
We prefer speed over size in our defense although we'd love to have both. Usually, for our defense to be successful, these players are "over-grown" linebackers. If they are all interchangeable it will make your defense more balanced, but if you have different skill sets here, is where we would play them.

Our "Anchor" is going to be a heavier and possibly slower defensive lineman. He will get double teamed more than any player on your defense.

Our "Bandit" is usually the most athletic defensive lineman as he will have chances to run plays down from the backside often.

Our "Nose" needs to either be able to 2-gap or be very quick and stunt to the strength of the offense. It would be best if he was a 2-gap player, but that is not often realistic at the high school level.

Defensive Line

We play 3 Defensive Linemen and look for a very similar build, but often that is not the case. Knowing that, we must often pick from what we are given. This is how we would adjust to what we have:

Anchor in our defense would be an athlete that will take on double teams and be willing to sacrifice for the team. While we would prefer a dominant player, we can work with an athlete willing to hold a gap and keep our linebackers free.

Bandit in our defense can often be an undersized quick lineman. This athlete is often under 6' tall for us, but willing to press flat down the line.

Nose in our defense can either be a dominant player that can 2-gap (that is the preference) or a quicker athlete that can cause a double team with his speed.

Inside Linebackers

Inside linebackers need to be great at running what we call the "horseshoe" or from A gap to C gap. While we would love to put a very athletic player here, we can work with at least one that has great instincts or is film study. This player must have a much higher "football IQ" than our defensive linemen as he is often reading keys and lining players up.

Our "Mike" needs to be more athletic and be able to cover in trips and often will need to cover in space.

Our "Sam" is the bigger of the two and must be able to fill inside on all runs. He is often also taking on lead blocks or pulling linemen. This player can be "hidden" in coverage, so that is lower on the skill set needed.

One, or both, of these players must be able to identify the offensive strength and get our defense in the correct front and call.

The Outside Linebacker position is one of the most crucial positions to fill in the 34 defense to be successful. We will always choose better athletes even if they are not ideal size for this position as it requires many skills at this position.

We will often play younger great athletes here as we groom them to become safeties as upperclassmen. We can also take DB type players to play here that may not be great in coverage or may be very aggressive.

Our "Will" often is more of a "nickel" in the 34. He often will be asked to play in space more than in the box.

Our "End" can be the same type of player, but it is best if he is a little larger and longer as he often will be asked to come down in a 9-technique and take on kickout blocks or lead backs.

Corners

In a perfect world corners are not made, they are born. In a perfect world these players would be our best athletes. Having great corners will enable you to bring more pressure and not need to give as much help with OLB's and others.

Since we do not always get to pick our players, we must adjust to this position's skill set more than any other position. For the defense to succeed it must adapt to the ability of the corners. If they are not able to play much man to man, we must work to give them help in our scheme. In this book, I walk through a few options to help them.

They must understand to keep people underneath them and how to play with great leverage.

Free Safety

This player will often be the best athlete on the defense. He must be able to tackle, cover and make calls and adjustments for our defense. For this defense to be successful we must put a great player in this spot.

If you have to make some concessions due to the ability or size of this player, make it with size. If he is a willing tackler and good in space, we can overlook a smaller player.

Dog

The Dog in my last 6 defenses has had over 100 tackles each season. Many years this player is our leading tackler. For this defense to work he is the "moving piece" that we use to get the numbers right in the passing and running game.

This player must be comfortable coming downhill and making tackles at the line of scrimmage, but also be comforatble making plays in the passing game 30-yards deep. He must be very durable as he will take a physical toll each game.

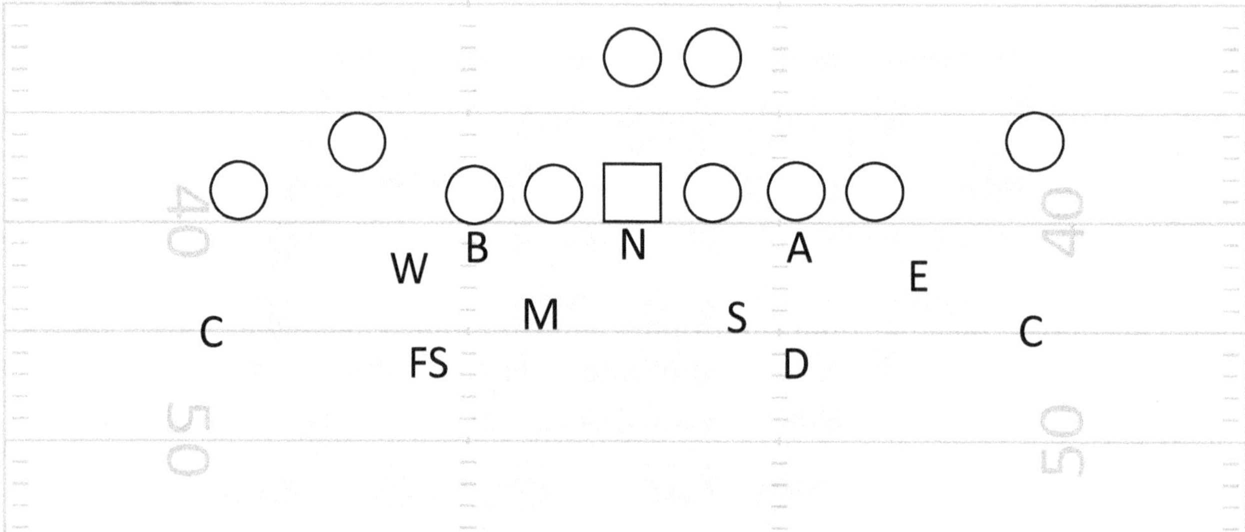

Position	PERSONNEL CHOICES
B	QUICKEST DEFENSIVE END
N	PERFER SPEED OVER SIZE. IF HE IS A PLUGGER, MAY BE A 2 GAP PLAYER
A	BIGGER OF THE D LINEMEN, WILL OFTEN GET DOUBLE TEAMED
W	ONE OF THE BEST ATHELETES, OFTEN THE 5TH DB
M	QUICKEST OF THE TWO INSIDE BACKERS
S	PLUGGER TYPE, MUST FIT THE RUN QUICKLY
E	BIGGER LB, "LONGER" BODY PREFERED
C	WORK WITH THE ABILITY, IF ONE IS BIGGER FLIP TO STRENGTH
FS	GENERALLY BEST COVER SAFETY OR TACKLING CORNER
D	BEST PLAYER ON THE TEAM
C	WORK WITH ABILITY IF, ONE IS BIGGER FLIP TO STRENGTH

Base Alignment

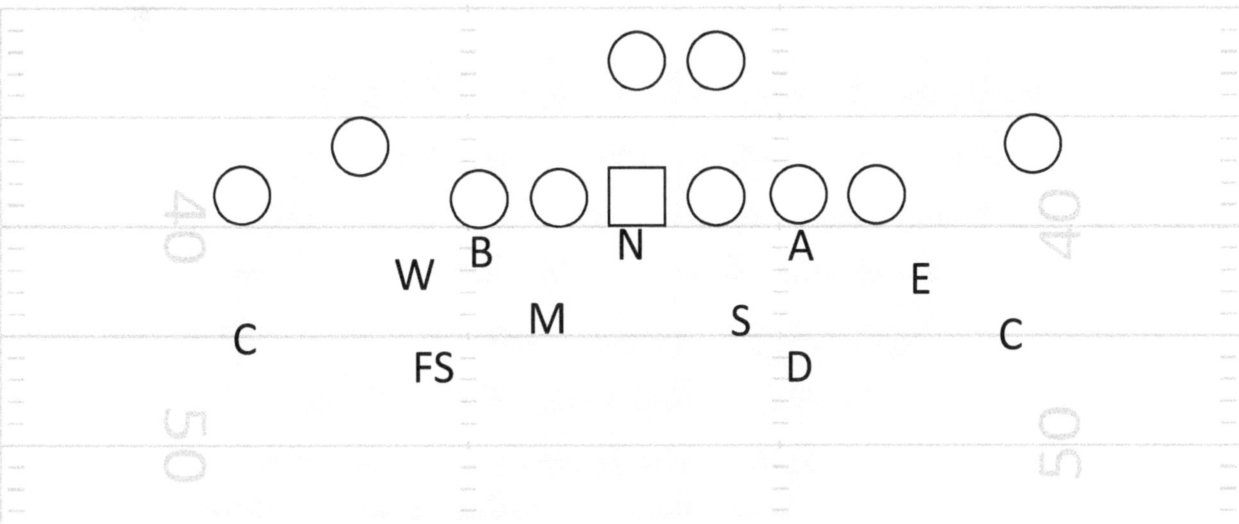

Position	PERSONNEL
B	Head up the tackle
N	Head up the center
A	Head up the tackle
W	Apex end man on the line and #2 WR
M	Outside Shade of Guard at 5 yards depth
S	Outside Shade of Guard at 5 yards depth
E	Dependent of formation – usually 2 x 2 off end man on the line
C	5-7 yards off by 1 yard inside
FS	7 yards – 2 yards inside #2 WR – Dependent on formation
D	7 yards - 2 yards inside #2 WR – Dependent on formation
C	5-7 yards off by 1 yard inside

FIND
A WAY

KENNY SIMPSON'S
FIT & SWARM
34 DEFENSE
A VERSATILE HIGH SCHOOL SYSTEM

Overview

OVERVIEW

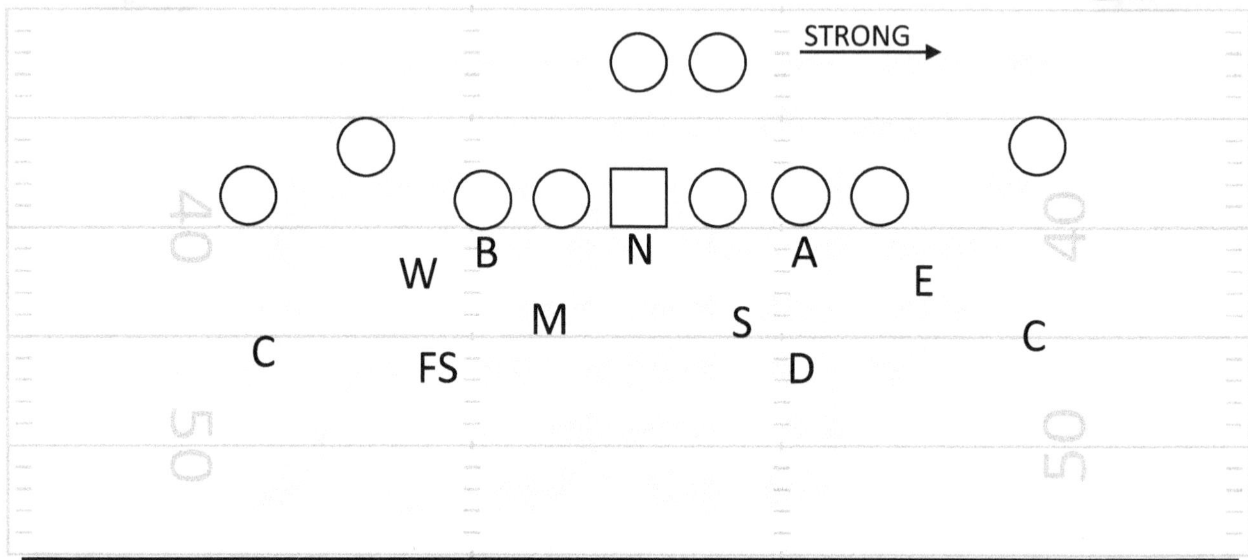

Position	BASE ALIGNMENTS
B	BASE ALIGN IN A 4 TECHINQUE
N	BASE ALIGN IN 0 TECHNIQUE
A	BASE AALIGN IN FOUR TECHNIQUE
W	BASE ALIGN IN A 9 TECHNIUQE 2-3 YARD DEPTH
M	BASE ALIGN IN "30" TECHNIQUE 5 YARD DEPTH
S	PASE ALIGN IN "30" TECHNIQUE 5 YARD DEPTH
E	BASE ALIGN IN A 9 TECHNIQUE 2-3 YARD DEPTH
C	INSIDE LEVERAGE OF #1 AT 6 YARD DEPTH
FS	INSIDE LEVERAGE OF #2 (NEVER MORE THAN 2 YARDS FROM HASH)
D	INSIDE LEVERAGE OF#2 (NEVER MORE THAN 2 YARDS FROM HASH)
C	INSIDE LEVERAGE #1 AT 6 YARDS DEPTH

Alignment Terms Defensive Line

GAPS

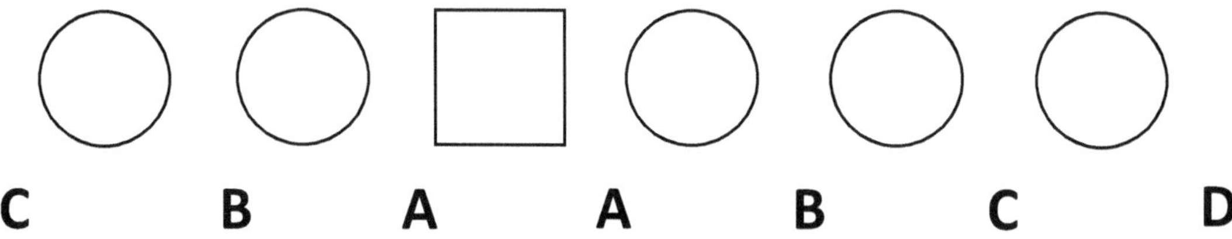

When teaching gaps to the defense we want to keep it is as simple as possible. We make sure each understands that for our defense to be successful we each must maintain our gap, but that these gaps are not stagnate. This is simply a starting point in understanding our responsibility.

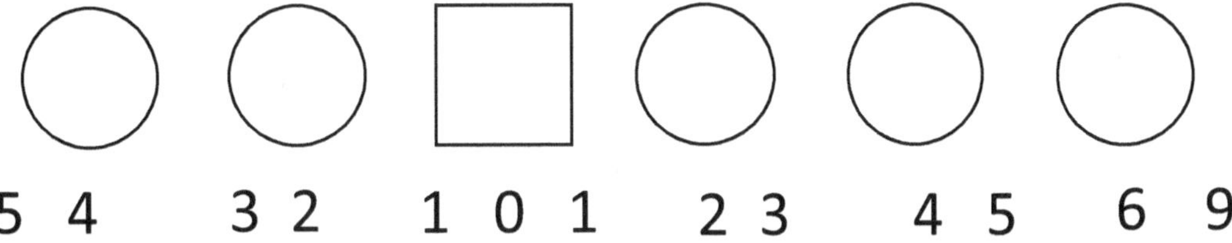

Working with our defensive linemen, we teach these as our "techniques". In most of our base concepts we are "head up" or in an even number. But we want the ability to move them at any point in time. It is simpler to teach them these numbers to help with alignment so that change can happen quickly and efficiently.

HEAD UP - RIP /LIZ

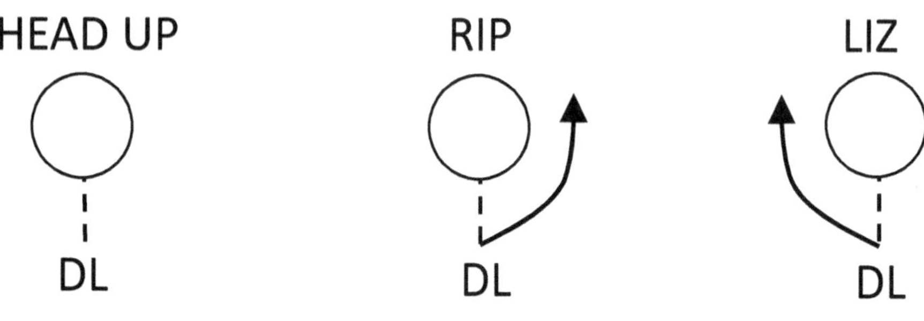

A few simple terms we use for our defensive line. Head up is as it sounds, line up nose-to-nose with the offensive lineman. If we want to move to the right regardless of strength we call "Rip". If we want the line to stunt to the left, we call "Liz" regardless of strength.

If we want to only stunt to the strength we call "slant," and our linebackers will automatically send them right/left depending on strength.

RIP CALL

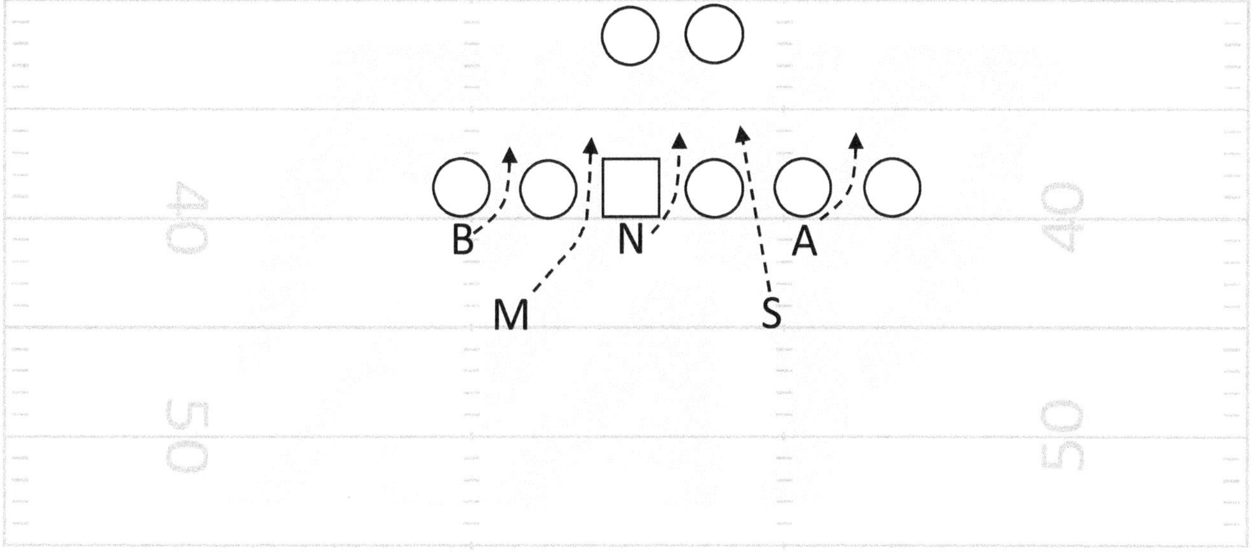

Position	Alignment - Assignment
B	ATTACKS B GAP
N	ATTACKS STRONG A GAP
A	ATTACK C GAP
M	ATTACKS A GAP
S	ATTACKS B GAP

LIZ CALL

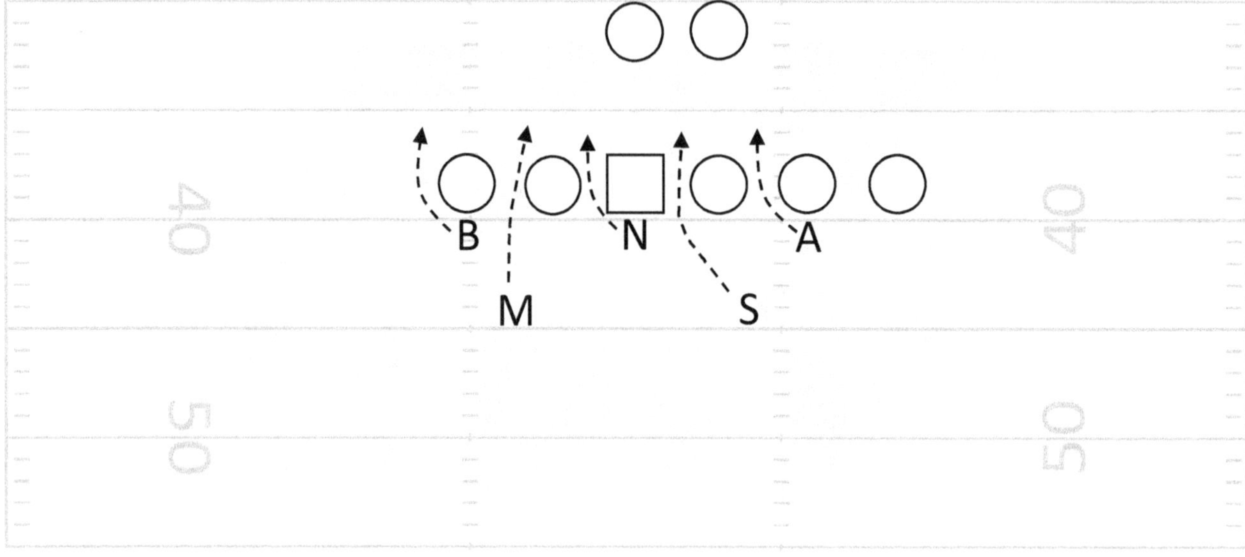

Position	Alignment - Assignment
B	ATTACKS C GAP
N	ATTACKS WEAK A GAP
A	ATTACK B GAP
M	ATTACKS B GAP
S	ATTACKS A GAP

PINCH/LOOP

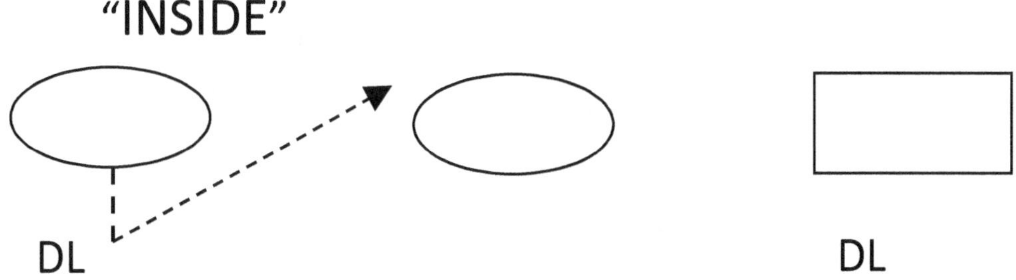

A "Pinch" call will send both our Anchor and Bandit into the "B" Gaps. We then teach to read the inside lineman as their key.

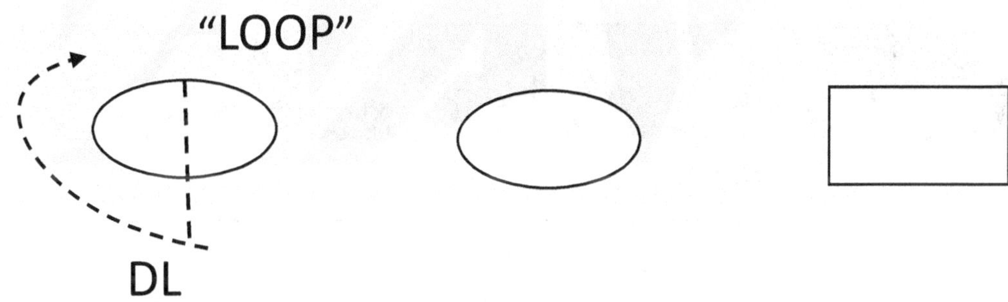

A Loop call will send both our Anchor and Bandit to the outside. This is often used in stunts with Linebackers or in passing downs.

PINCH CALL

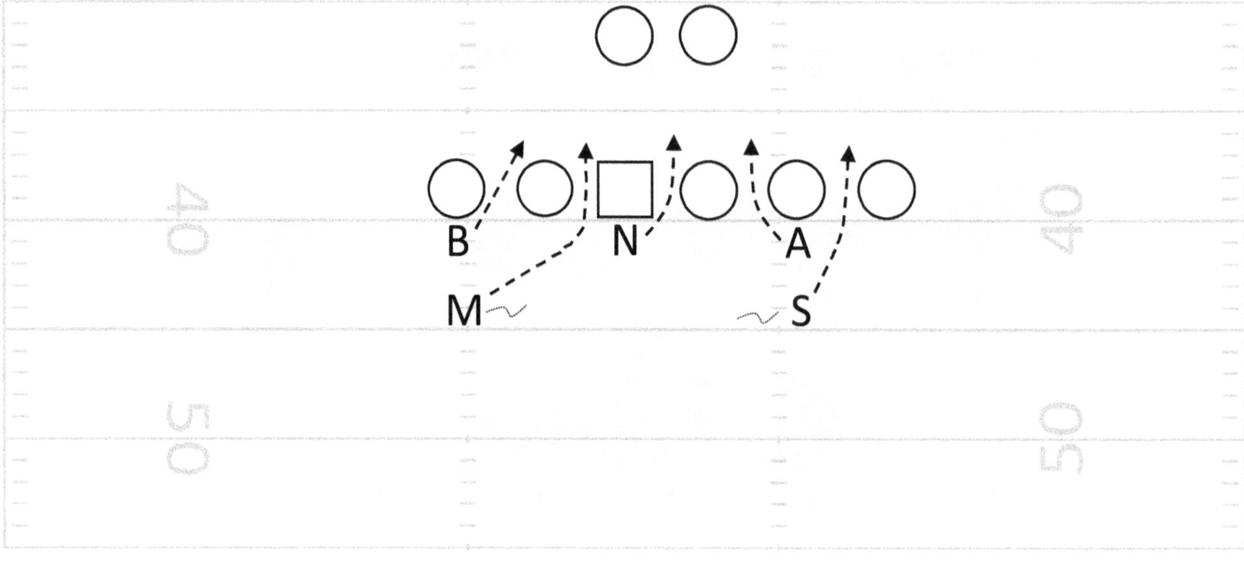

Position	Alignment - Assignment
B	ATTACKS B GAP
N	PINCH CALL CAN 2 GAP OR STRONG A GAP
A	ATTACK B GAP
M	“40” ALIGNMENT - ATTACK A GAP
S	“40” ALIGNMENT - ATTACK C GAP

In our defensive system we teach our defensive lineman to read the headgear of the offensive lineman they are playing the gap from. While we do not often line up in a "5 technique", we like to start from this spot to learn how to read our keys.

As with this entire system, we attempt to keep it simple. So, we will give our players 3 keys:

1) If the lineman fires into you and "base" blocks – Press him back into the hole and attempt to cross his face if possible.

2) If the lineman pulls – Get in his "hip pocket" and follow down the line as flat as possible.

3) If we read a pass set – we will rush our gap unless the "window" opens on the inside and then we can attack either way to the QB.

Keeping with our simple rules we want our defensive lineman to know these basic principles:

STAY FLAT – Do not come up-field more than a yard, unless we read a pass.

Follow your keys at full speed – If we are wrong, move fast and stay flat.

Get our hands on the offensive lineman we are keying – Do not allow them a free release to our Linebackers.

We do not have to worry about containment unless we are given a "Loop" call.

Calling Strength

Calling Strength

One of the most important things a defense can do is to line up correctly each snap. It is often assumed athletes can do this, but in my experience even at the highest level it can be difficult to line up correctly. We attempt to give our athletes a few simple rules to get us lined up.

While we seek to be balanced and able to handle shifts and trades, we want to do our best to get the best matchup possible. Our basic rules of strength:

1) To the TE (or 3-man surface)
2) To the FB/H-back (can change depending on film)
3) To the "Lesser WR" side
4) Away from better runner in the backfield
5) To the field

As with anything, it can and will change depending on our opponent breakdown, but this gives our athletes some base rules to be able to line up as well as possible.

STRENGTH CALL EXAMPLES

RULES FOR FRONT CALL FRONT 7

**BACK 4 ARE DIVORCED FROM CALL **

STRONG →

1. TE

STRONG →

2. FB AWAY

STRONG →

3. FEWER WR'S

STRONG ←

4. AWAY FROM THE BETTER RUNNER
5. FIELD

STRONG

(1) TE

STRONG

(2) FB AWAY

(3) FEWER WIDE RECIEVERS

STRONG →

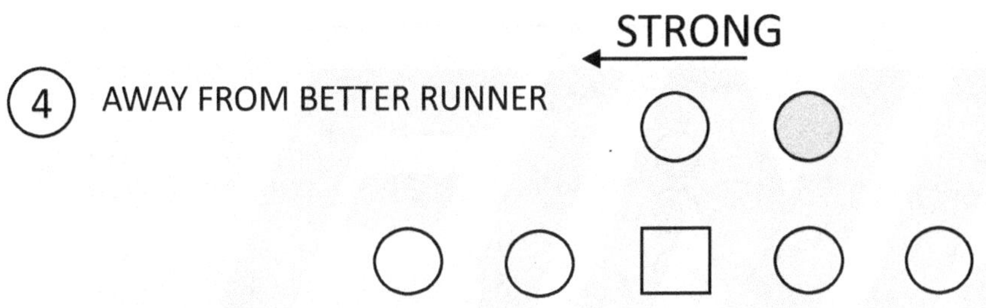

(5) WIDE SIDE OF THE FIELD

SETTING STRENGTH

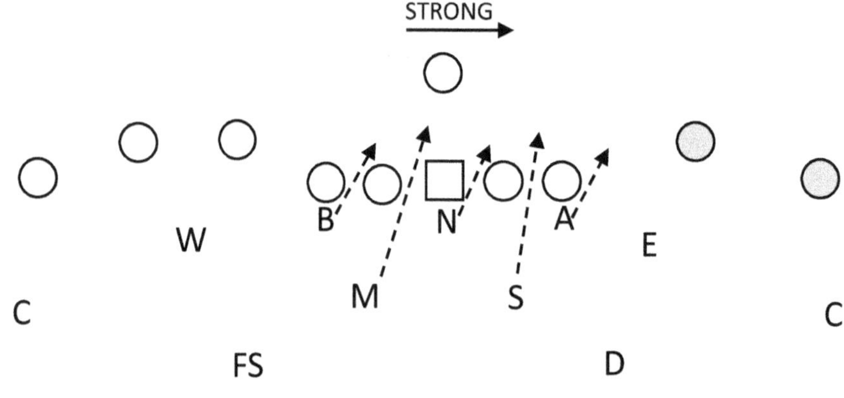

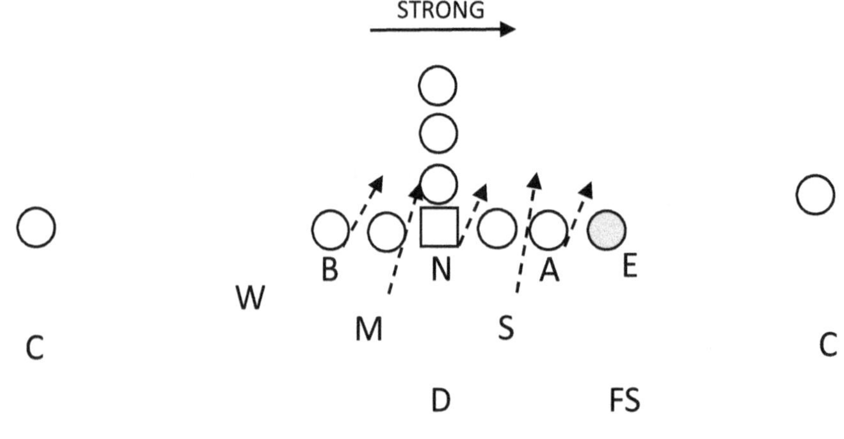

SETTING STRENGTH

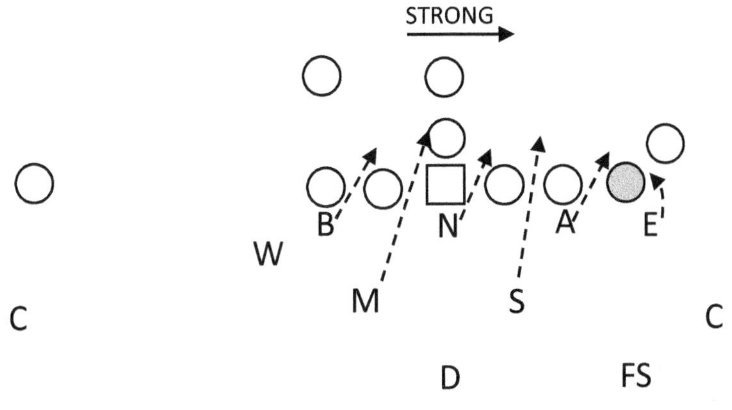

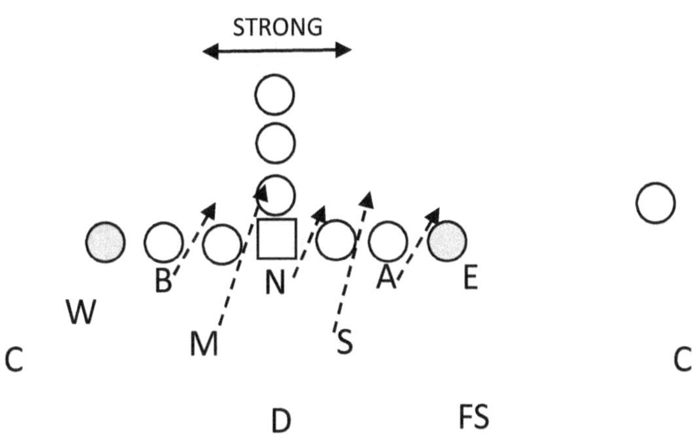

SETTING STRENGTH

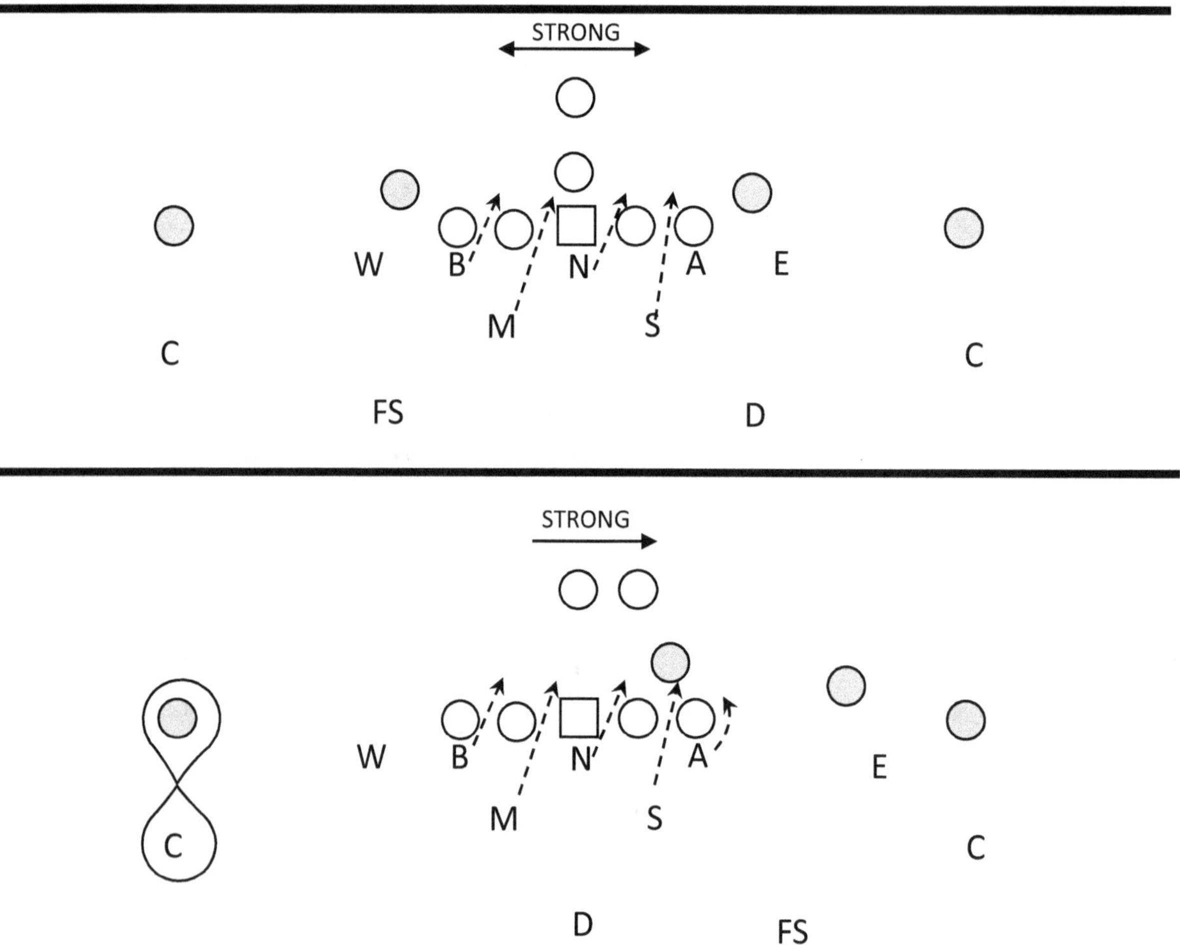

SETTING STRENGTH

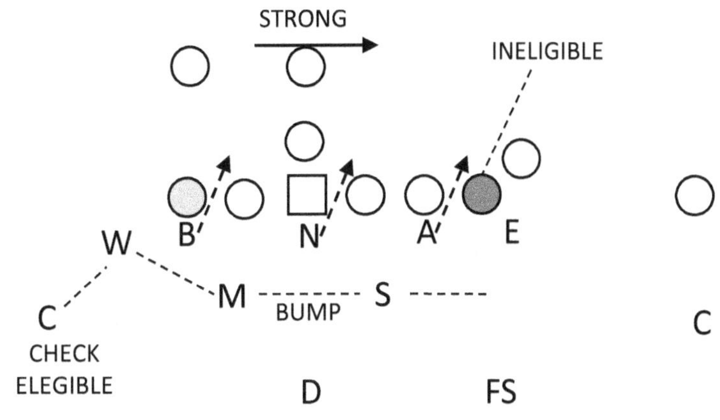

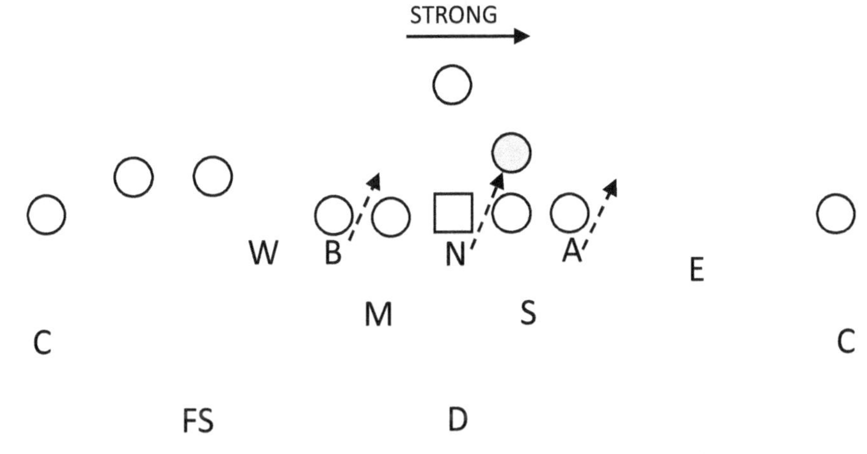

FIND
WAY

KENNY SIMPSON'S
FIT & SWARM
34 DEFENSE
A VERSATILE HIGH SCHOOL SYSTEM

Alignment & Keys
Back Eight

LB TECHNIQUES

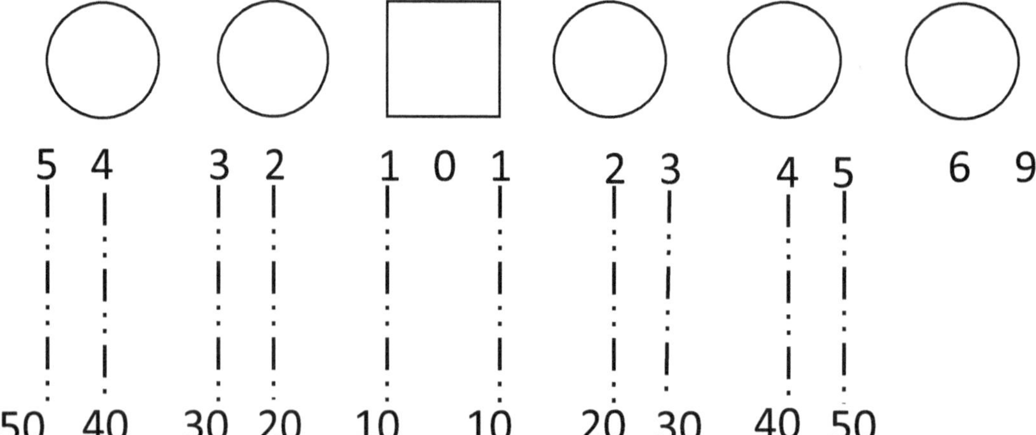

Our defense is simple. We want our players to be able to move back or down on the defensive line if they are able. By keeping our alignment numbers close to the same, we make it simple for our players. So, a "3" technique for a defensive lineman is a "30" for a linebacker.

While we often do not communicate with these numbers, it makes it easier for us to make quick in-game adjustments if needed.

Inside Linebacker Keys

We want our Inside Linebackers to move efficiently. While we will adjust keys each week with them, we generally will give them a single read each week.

We want them to fit from "C" gap to "C" gap and play with inside leverage – meaning they track the inside hip of the ball carrier – at all times. As a coaching staff, you must adjust a few things we due to your personnel:

1) How will you take on blocks from lineman – we will allow the "dip and rip" with smaller quicker players. If the linebacker is larger, we will teach anchoring in the hole.

2) Alignment – We will play them wider and deeper if they are less athletic to help them from space.

3) Making the front calls – One of these players must be able to communicate to the defensive linemen and get our front set. It can be the "Mike" or the "Sam".

Rules of ILB

Base rules for our Inside Linebackers:

1) We will run the "horseshoe" or play the inside hip at all times.

2) We want to make all runners "spill" to our OLB/Safety

3) We want to look to "shoot through windows" and "scrape by closed doors". Meaning we will attack through an open gap, but do not want to run into the back of our linemen.

4) We will often teach "delayed pressure" with our "Sam" to the QB if he reads pass. This often creates a natural gap that he will shoot

One of the most important aspects of Outside Linebacker play is to line up correctly. These next few pages show how we teach our alignment rules to OLB. By teaching the all the basic scenarios we can get them lined up to almost any offensive formation.

While this will take some time early, it will be worth the investment. In the 34 system the OLB play and alignment is one of the most important aspects. We teach our players that in order to be successful the first step is getting lined up correctly.

APEX

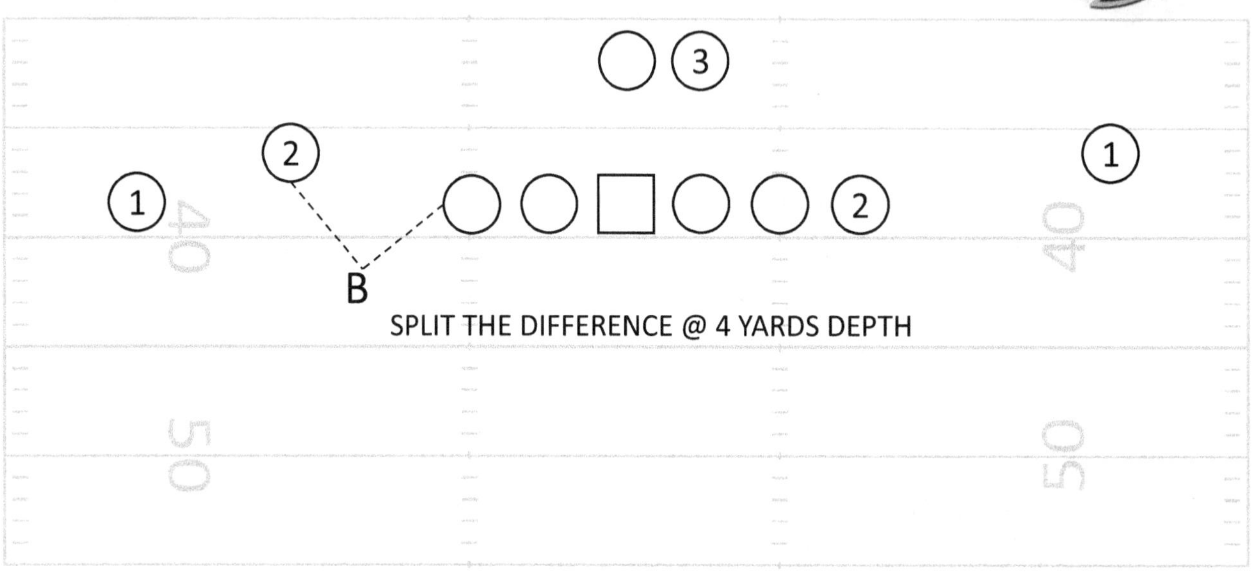

The first formation to teach is a basic 2 WR set. We would "APEX" this formation and split the difference between the OT and the #2 WR. We teach this at 3-4 yards depth.

"APEX" TRIPS

APEX FROM #2 AND #3
3 YARDS DEPTH

Lining up to trips is important in today's football. We teach multiple methods to cover trips, but our base alignment is for our Outside Linebacker to "APEX" between the #2 and #3 WR.

PLAYING BUNCH

"JAM" OUTSIDE LEVERAGE
OF POINT MAN

Bunch formations are becoming more and more prevalent in the spread world. We work with out Outside Linebackers on disrupting the WR and keeping outside leverage in the run game. This is our "Jam" technique.

ALIGN OLB

1 BASE

1

2

B

PLAY 9 TECHNIQUE

When we play more traditional teams, we have a few ways to work on aligning to a TE. The first few things we ask in the gameplan:

1) Is the TE a blocking or receiving threat?

2) Are they better at kicking out OLB's or blocking them in space?

Our base alignment is a "9-Technique".

BOX TECHNIQUE

(2) BOX

PLAY 9 TECHNIQUE FROM
4 YARDS DEPTH

We use our "Box" call to get our OLB off the ball and in space where he is harder to block. We want to maintain outside leverage but play from depth.

HOLD TECHNIQUE

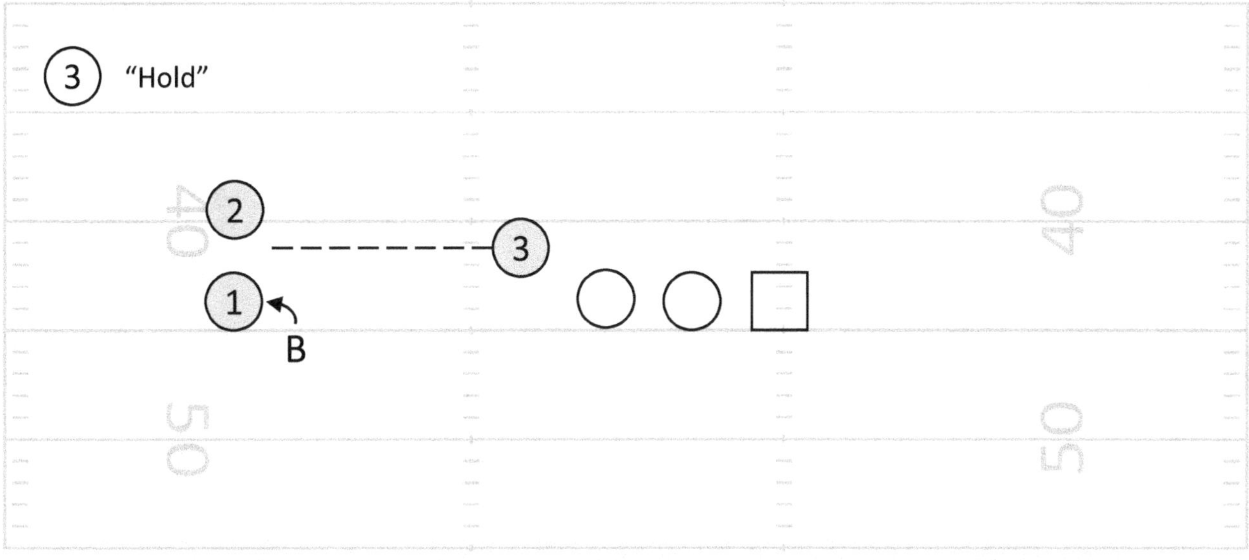

Our "hold" technique is one way we attempt to double cover an opponent's best player. This is something we keep in our playbook for when we take on a very talented player.

OLB RUN FIT

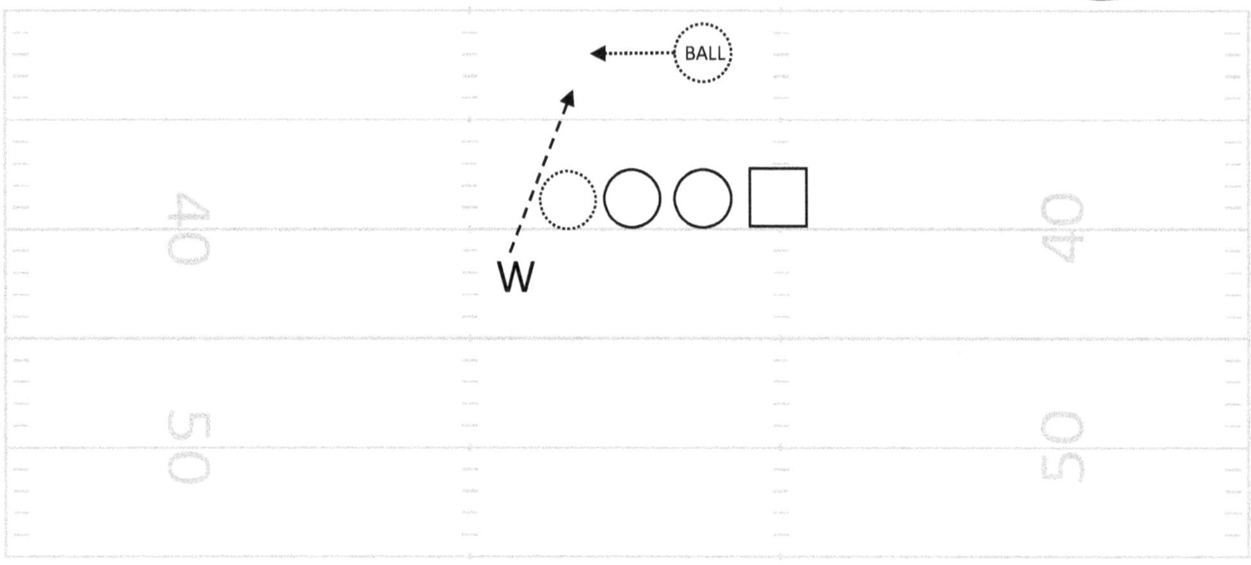

Teaching our Outside Linebackers simple techniques has allowed them to play fast and sound defense. In this section I will go through the run fits we give them and the base pass coverage rules.

In this first one the ball carrier is heading to them. We teach an "outside hip" leverage - staying on the outside hip of the ball carrier and forcing a cut back. Depending on the skill level of our OLB we will allow him to line up tighter if he is able to maintain outside leverage as it will condense the space. If he is new to the position, we want him to line up wider to give him a cheat.

OLB RUN FIT

BALL

W

If the ball goes away – we teach a slow fit watching for a reverse, boot, or cutback. One way to teach this is to tell our OLB's to "take a picture" before pursuing. This is the only time we do not want the "SWARM" mentality as they must stay home for any counter action from the offense.

OLB COVERAGE "SINGLE"

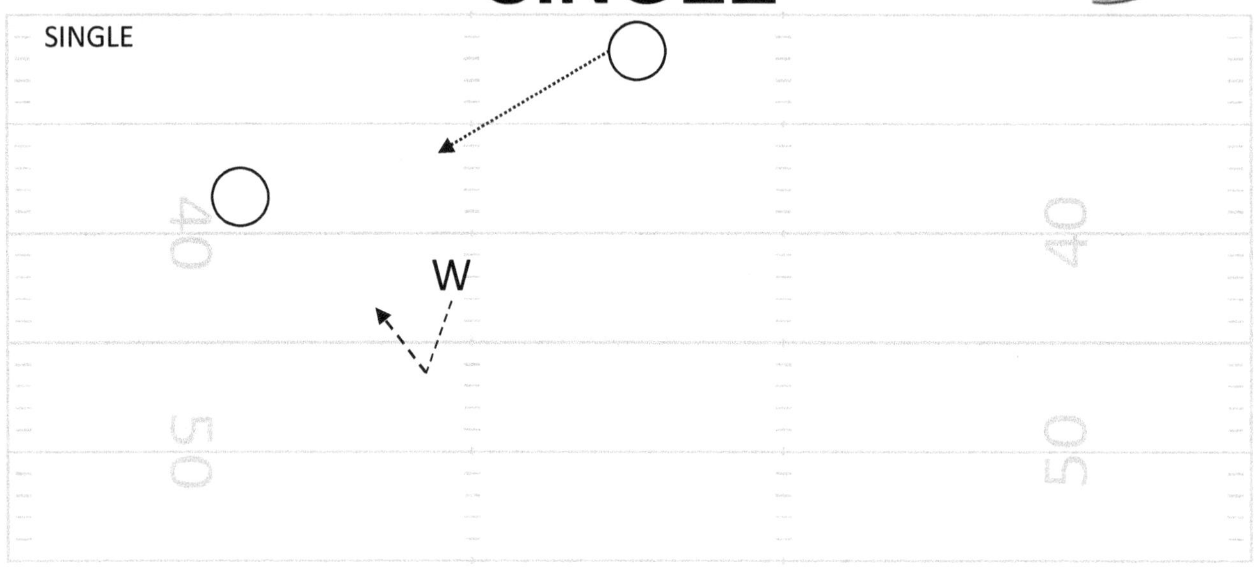

When lined up with a single WR we ask our Outside Linebackers to take away inside routes and screen passes. This allows our corners to play off and react to inside breaking routes. While we have a few calls that can change this up for the offense, this is our base rule.

We don't ever want to "Spot drop". We simply teach to deny the slant/curl and react to hitches and out routes. We want our eyes on the WR after we read pass.

"BOX" CALL

I put this diagram to show that we will teach the same technique with our WR's as when we line up in our base. Even if we have "box" called to help with the run game, if we read pass, we expect our OLB to turn and find the WR and deny slants/digs/curls.

OLB COVERAGE "TWINS"

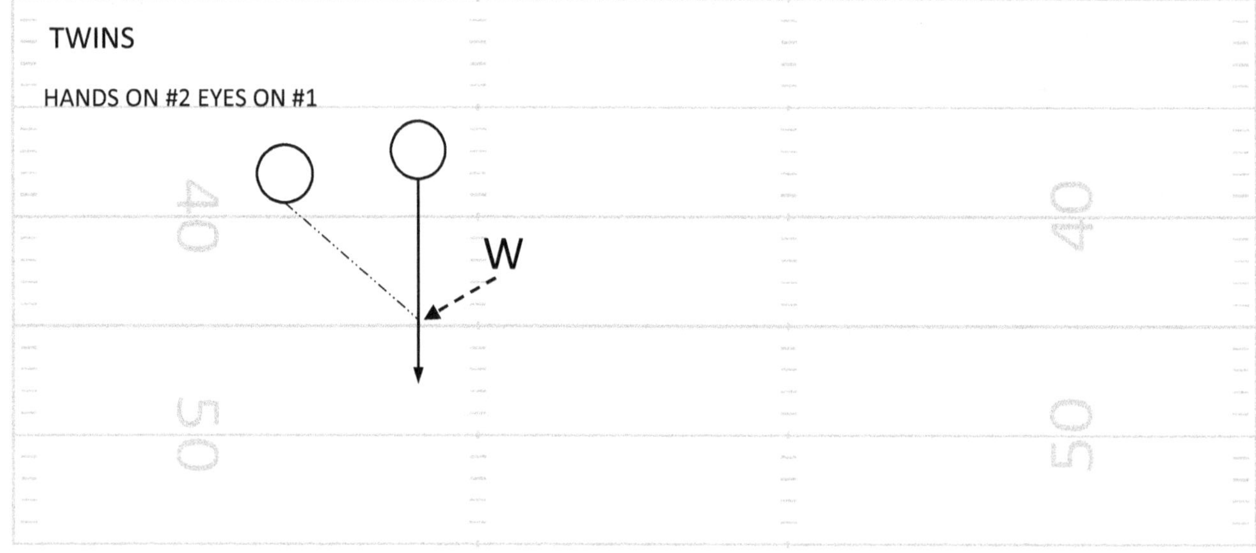

When we have twins to our side, we teach a "hands on 2 and eyes on 1" concept. Again, we do not spot drop. We want to always see the routes developing. In order we want to deny:

1) Seam/Hitch Routes by #2
2) Dig/Slant by #1

We also want to get contact on the WR to slow his speed as he is often working on a safety.

OLB COVERAGE "TRIPS"

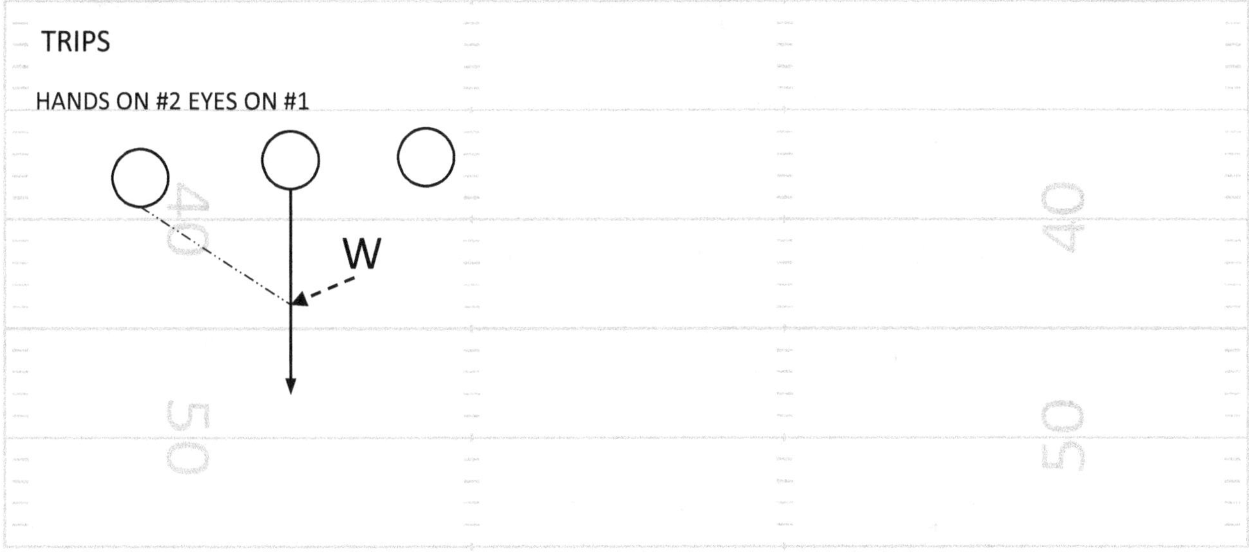

While we have a few adjustments to trips, our base coverage is to play the exact same as we would with twins. We want to have "hands on 2 and eyes on 1" and would react late to a chute route by #3.

OLB Rules

When teaching our Outside Linebackers, we attempt to live by a rule of 3. That way they can react quickly and decisively. I often tell them they are "safeties with no consequences". They can gamble to make plays as long as they maintain these 3 rules:

1) If the run comes to me – attack the outside hip of the ball carrier and avoid all blocks by keeping outside arm free.

2) If the run goes away – "take a picture" and slow play for cutback/reverse

3) If it is a pass – find the WR's in my area and gamble on all slants/curls/screens.

We will adjust based on our ability level, but these three rules do not change for our defense to be successful.

DB Play

One of the hardest positions to play in all of football, especially on the defensive side of the ball, is defensive back. These players' mistakes are always magnified and turn into points for the opposition. To that end, we try to keep some basic simple rules for this position, and we always tailor our game plan or adjust our alignment based on this position's ability level.

The years we have had our best defenses this area was a strength, so I would suggest starting your defensive selections at safety each year. This position, as well as corner, will be the key to your success on the defensive side of the ball.

In this section I am going through our base rules and alignment, but understand we are very willing to adjust based on what talent our players have. If we have a strong corner, we will allow them to line up inside and closer to WR's. If he is young or limited, we tend to back them up more and play outside leverage with help from an OLB.

ALIGN DB' & CORNERS

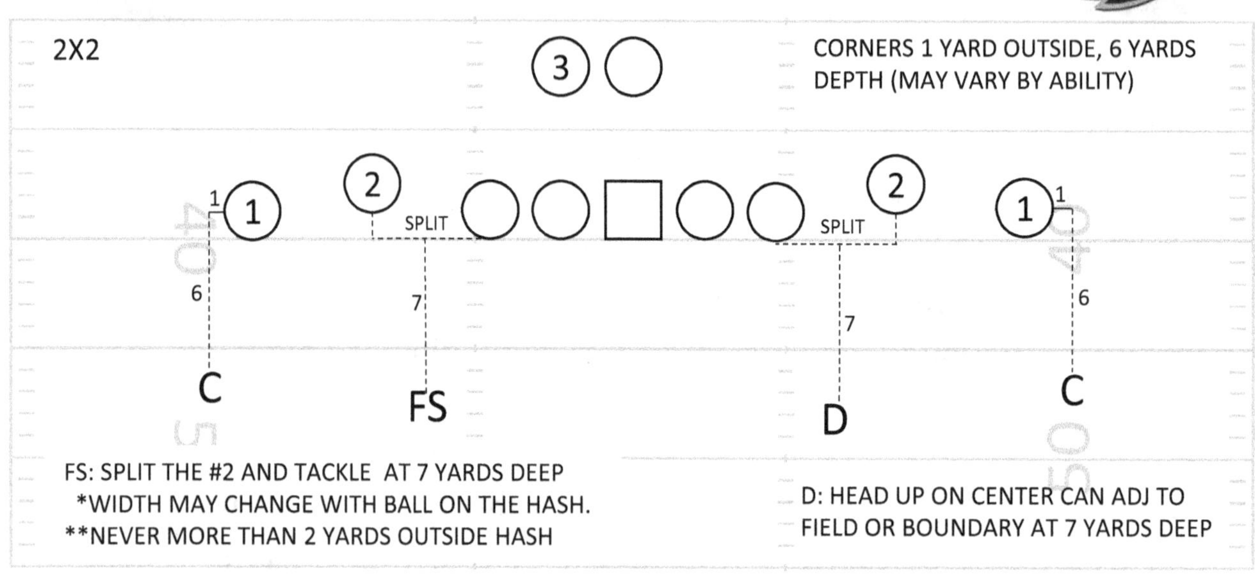

Base alignment for DB's in our 34 defense.

*If our corners are more experienced, then we will allow them to line up head up to even slightly inside of #1. Starting with outside leverage is easier for them to "pattern read".

In a perfect world we would like to be at the same depth to hide our coverage, but often we must adjust to our ability level. We do want both safeties at the same depth, whether that is 7-10 yards.

SAFETY RUN FITS

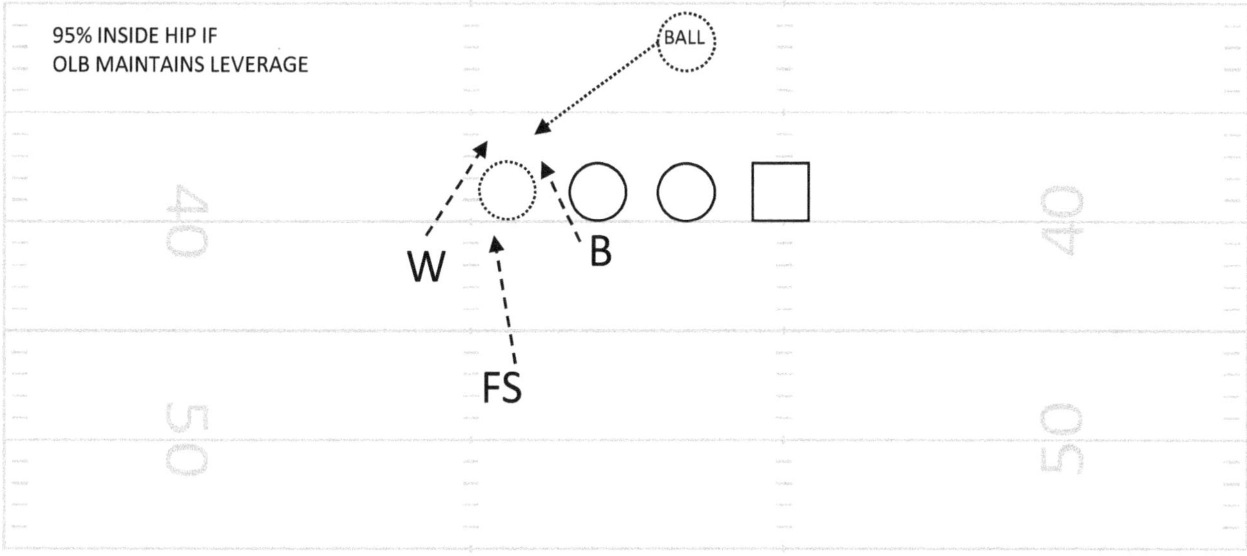

We tell our safeties that their job is to make the Outside Linebackers "right" in the run fit. They need to start off tracking the inside hip of the ball carrier and this is how we would like the fit to look.

OLB on outside hip and safety filling the alley.

SAFETY RUN FITS

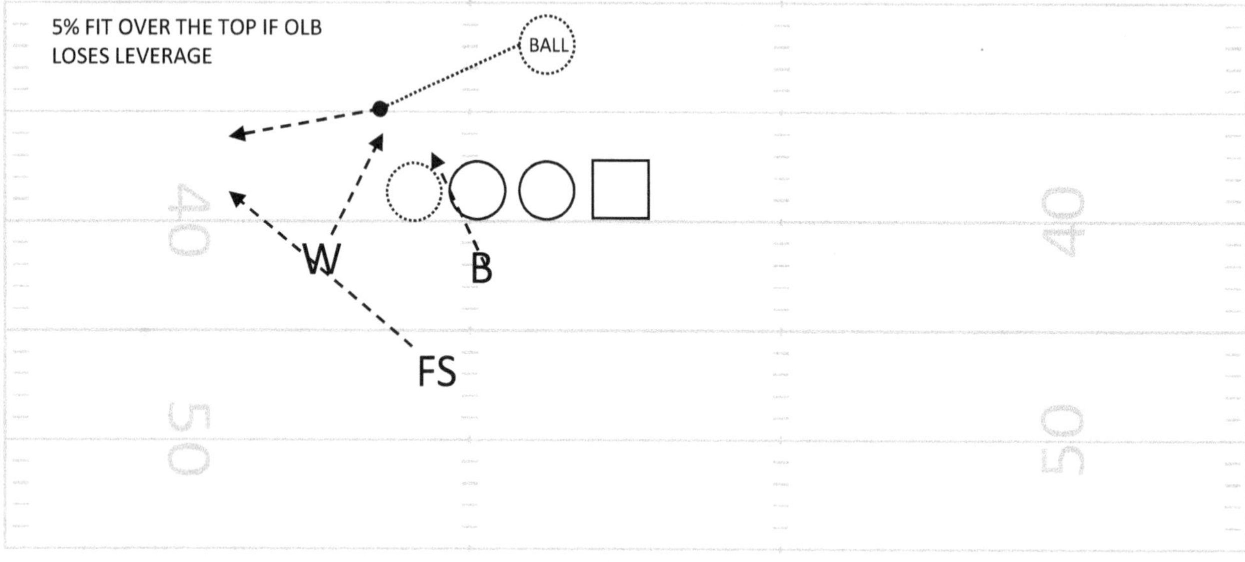

Again, we tell our safeties that their job is to make the Outside Linebackers "right" in the run fit. Often this happens in the run game when an OLB has forced the ball to spill and not kept contain.

Our safety can generally see this coming early in a play as the OLB will be fitting tight and there is no alley to fill. This means the ball will more than likely spill and he must track that direction.

Free Safety Rules

As with each position we give some simple rules to our positions. Safety is more complex than most of our positions, and that is why we tend to play a more experienced player or a very "football savy" player at this spot. Here are the base rules we teach him:

1) Do not give up inside leverage in the run or pass game – ever. If he can force the ball out wide, he will have help with a corner and possibly and OLB, but if the ball gets inside of him, he has no help.

2) Keep eyes on #2 WR for his pattern read, but do not chase him.

3) He must recognize all eligible receivers and communicate that to the back 8.

Dog Rules

Our Dog is probably our most versatile player as he often is "in the box" but must be able to play coverage. We attempt to keep his rules simple also.

1) If he has a 2 x 2 or Empty set, he will play our "base coverage". Otherwise, he is often in the box and keying an H-back or Tight End.

2) We want him to back pedal vs. WR's and play flat footed vs. backfield players/Tight Ends.

3) He is an inside hip player on run game but must make the OLB and ILB's fits right. Basically, fit through the natural alley that will develop during the play.

CORNER RUN FITS

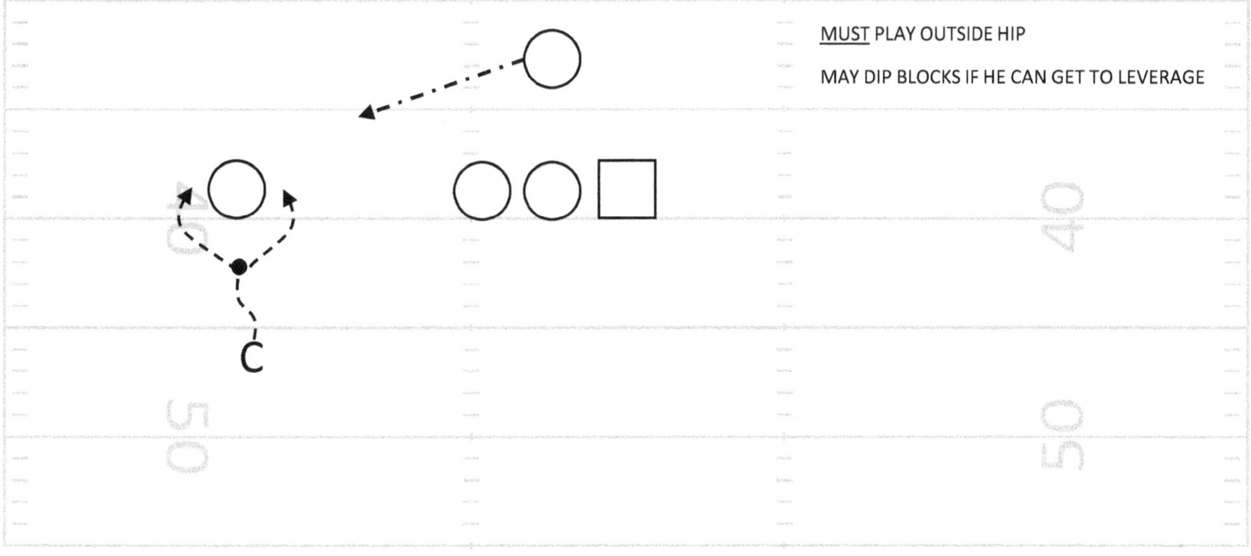

While we select our corners based on their ability to cover, they must be willing tackers in our defense for it to function at a high level. We teach outside leverage against all runs. The only time a corner would play the inside hip is if they were using the sideline as an extra defender.

We do allow them to dip and chute through alleys if they are 100% sure they can get there and maintain outside leverage on the ball carrier.

CORNER PASS READS

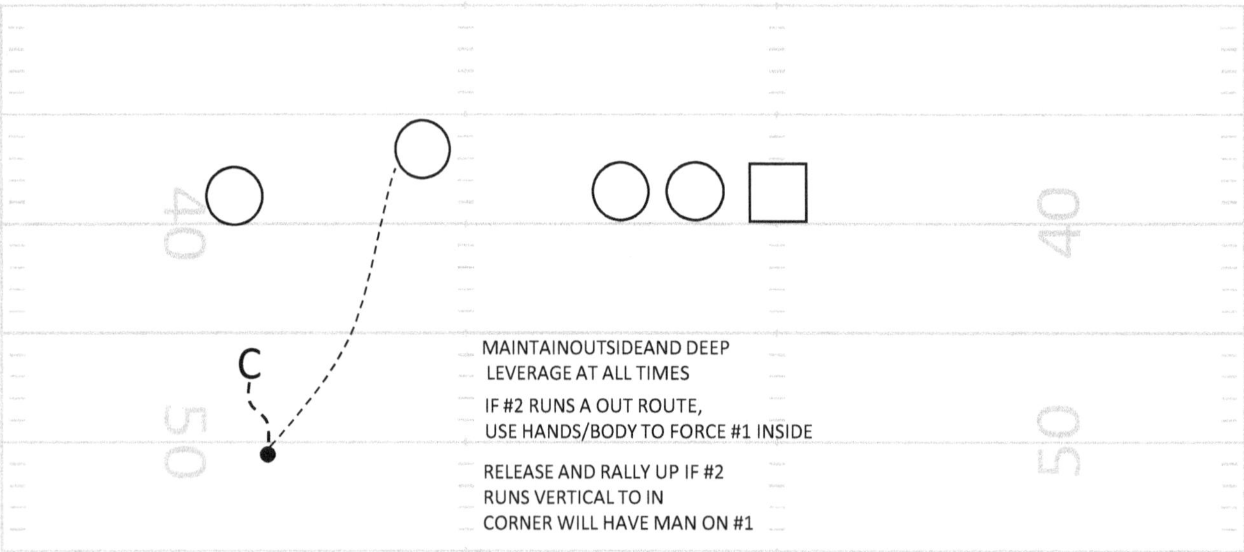

We have a few concepts in coverage, but our base coverage is patter read cover 2 or “Palms” as many coaches call it. Basically, our corner would read the #2 WR, and if he runs any route to the flats, he runs through the outside of the #1 WR to cover it.

We want to get “hands on 1 and eyes on 2” as the routes develop.

We want to always maintain deep leverage and outside leverage on all verticals/corner routes or other deep breaking routes.

If unsure, keep getting depth and width.

Corner Rules

As with each position, we want our rules to be very simple for our corners.

1) Maintain deep and outside leverage if we are unsure of what is happening. We can always make a tackle if the ball is in front of us.

2) Do not let any ball carrier outside of us.

3) If we have a single – know where (or if) our help is coming from.

FIND
WAY

KENNY SIMPSON'S
FIT & SWARM
34 DEFENSE
A VERSATILE HIGH SCHOOL SYSTEM

Front Calls and Alignment

SLANT

Earlier in this book I went through our "rip/liz" calls. Those are the first ones we put in for our defense. Once they understand the basic idea of movement and gaps, we start to give them some other calls – Pinch, Loop, etc…

When the LB's begin to recognize strength, we prefer to use the "SLANT" call. This is telling them we will "Rip/Liz" to the strength of the formation. This is much better to use in the game as it will always stunt your front to the strength if that is what you feel will benefit the team.

We then teach another word for "Weak SLANT" or to move them to the weak side of the formation.

All of this is dependent on the Inside Linebackers understanding strength and the game plan. If they are able to do so, we prefer to use SLANT.

SLANT

BASE

STRONG

SLANT

B N A
W E
M S
C C
FS D

BASE

STRONG

SLANT

B N A E
W
M S
C C
FS D

FIND WAY

SLANT

KENNY SIMPSON'S
FIT & SWARM
34 DEFENSE
A VERSATILE HIGH SCHOOL SYSTEM

BASE
SLANT
STRONG
B
N
A
E
W
C
M
S
C
FS
D

BASE
SLANT
STRONG
B
N
A
W
E
C
M
S
C
FS
D

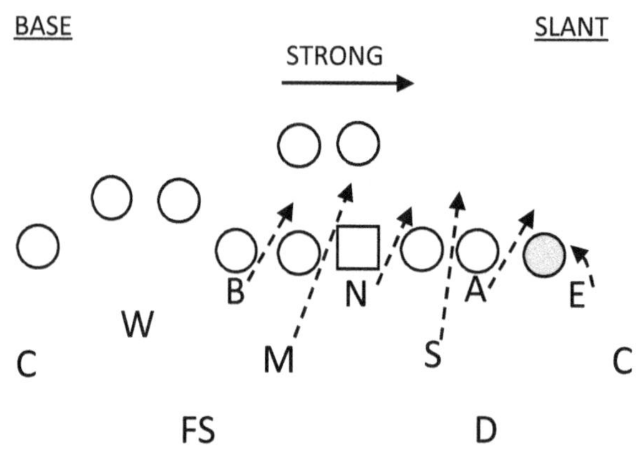

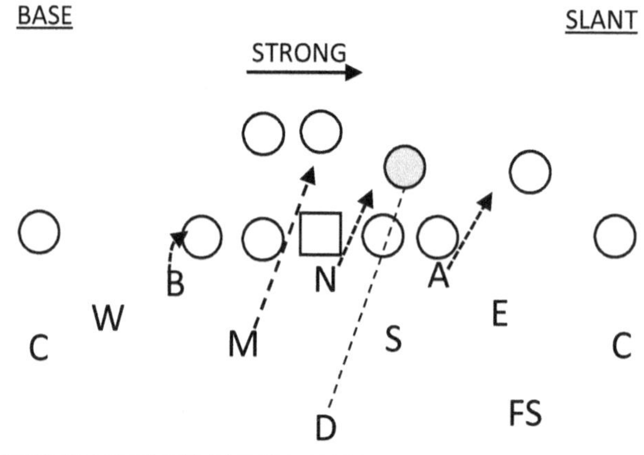

FRONTS

WIDE

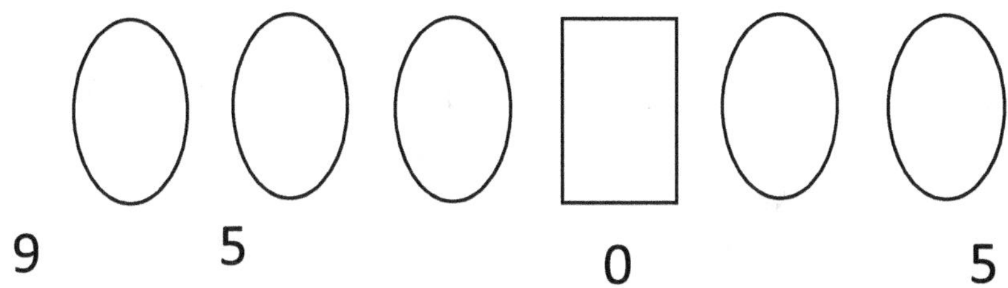

20 30

BEAR

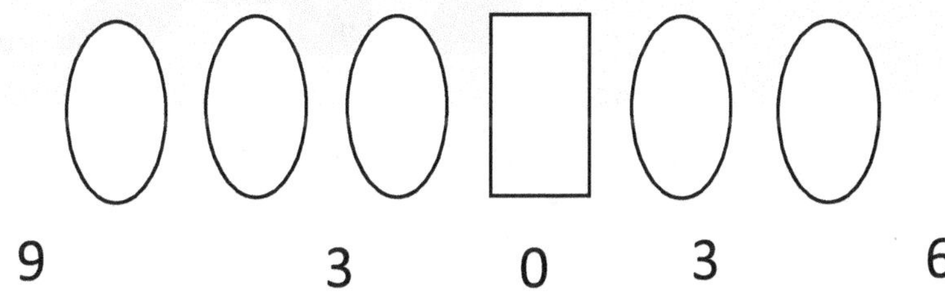

40 40

Base Alignment

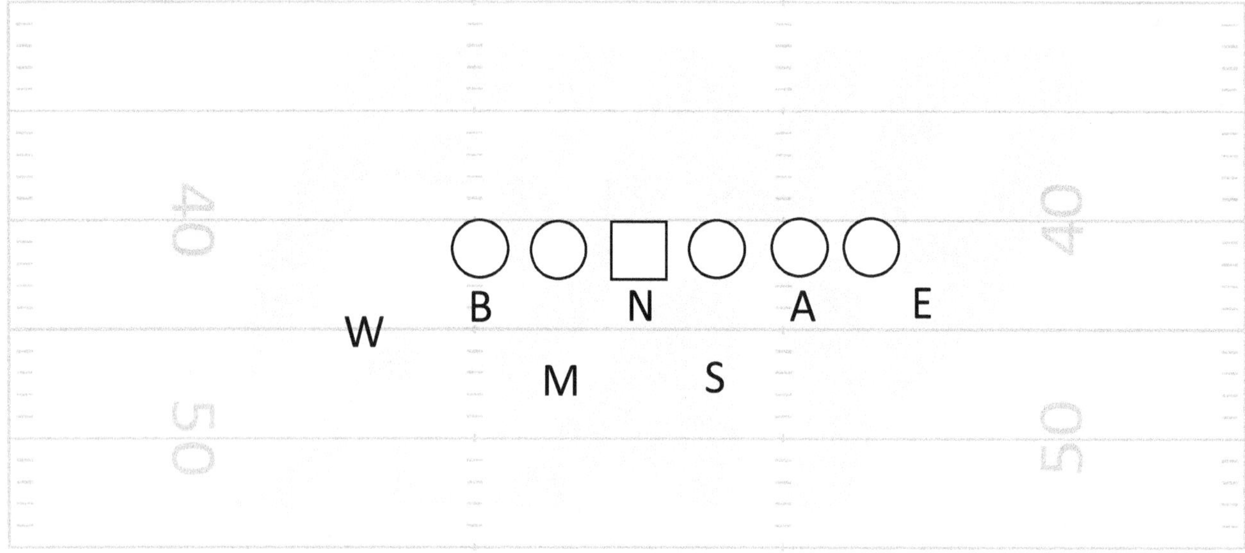

This is what our "Base" alignment would be to an offensive front. We want to line up "head" up with our Defensive Line and this would be our Outside Linebackers base rules for alignment.

We would then call our movement by using one of our tag words.

"Bear" Front

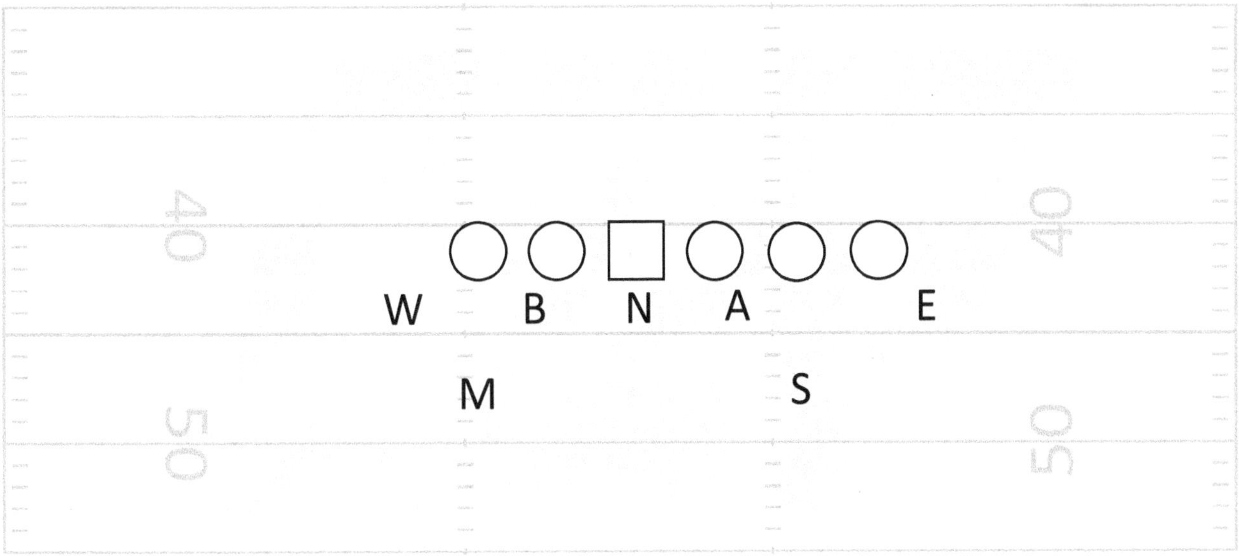

We have a few other tags for lining up differently if we feel our movement is not working or we want to give a different look. This is our "Bear" front.

We have condensed our Defensive line to a 3-0-3 look. We have also widened our Inside Linebackers as they will need to cover a wider gap.

"Wide" Front

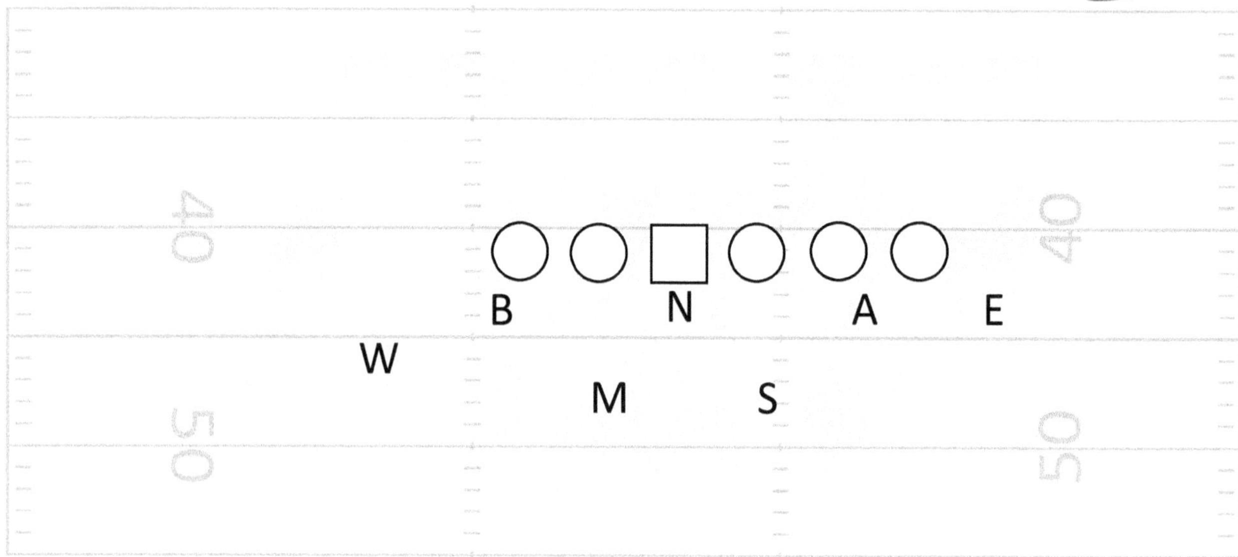

We also have a "Wide" look. Often we will come up with a name for this set – IE: "War" and even use different personnel groupings.

This is a set we would prefer to rush the passer or near the end of the half/game.

Adjusting to Overload

OVER

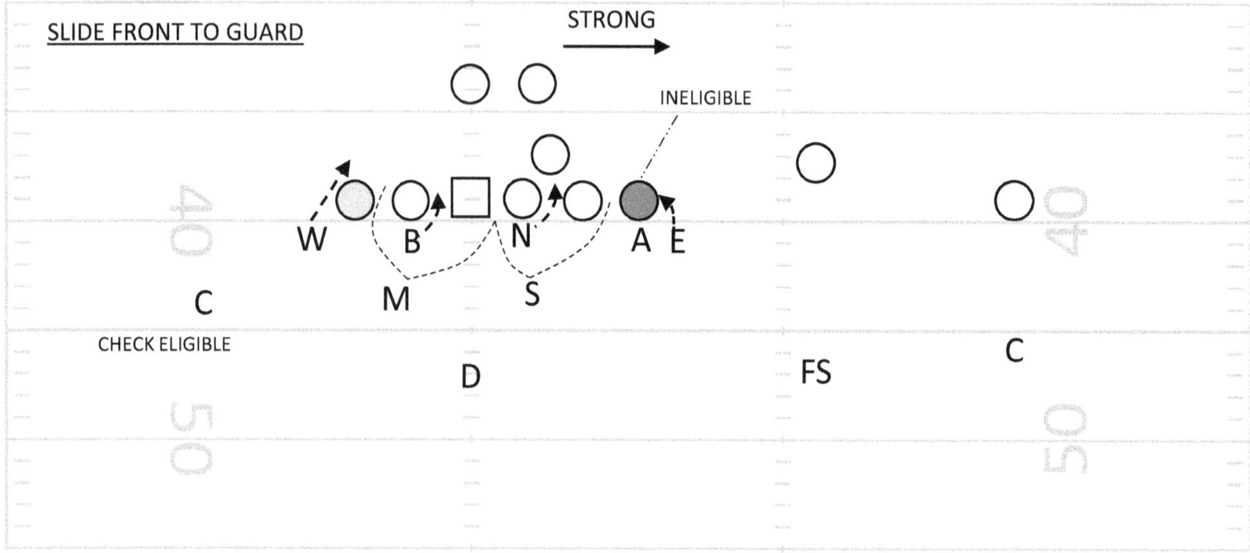

As with any defense, you must have a simple check to "over" looks or unbalanced looks. We attempt to follow a few simple rules for over sets as a base look. If we play a team that uses them often, we will have multiple looks, but we always want to be prepared for these odd looks.

1) If it is an unbalanced look with the line, we will line up with our line (as is shown in the picture).

2) If it is an unbalanced look with WR's we will adjust with our DB/LB group.

Coverages

Coverages
Base

WIDE RECIEVER COUNT

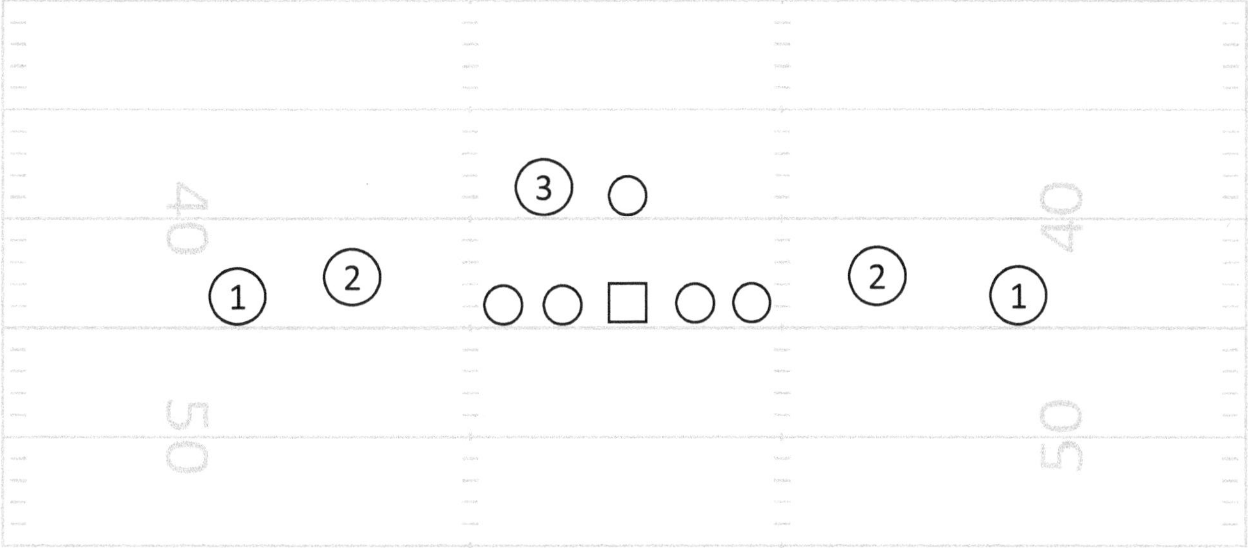

Teaching to count WR's should be a simple task and is important. We always want to work from outside in and identify all eligible WR's.

We teach –
1) There can never be more than 4 eligible on one side.
2) Always look to find at least 1 eligible even if they are on the line of scrimmage.

INSIDE LEVERAGE

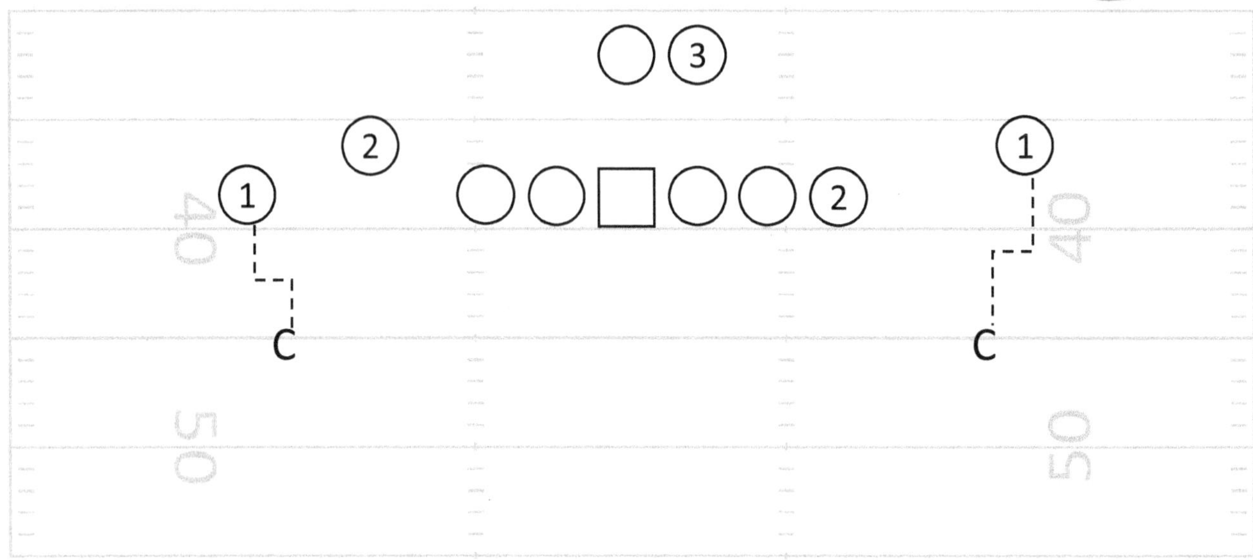

Inside leverage simply means taking away inside routes by alignment for us on defense. Here is an example of our corners in inside leverage.

OUTSIDE LEVERAGE

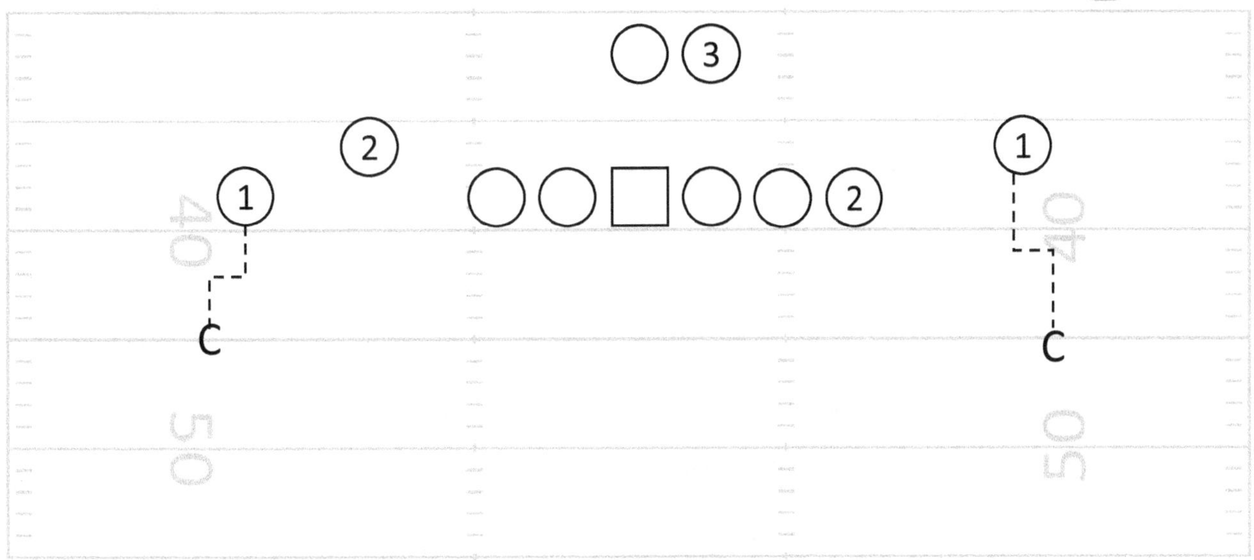

Outside leverage means taking away all outside breaking routes by alignment. In this diagram, we are lining up our corners in outside leverage.

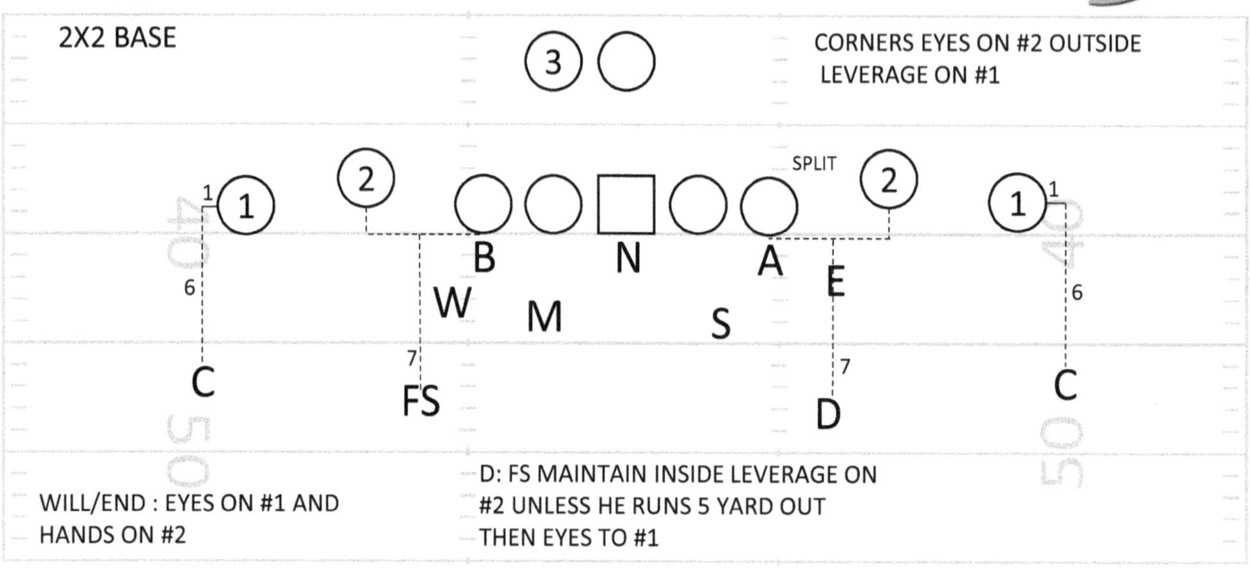

Day 1 alignment for us would be outside leverage with our corners. As they gain experience, we may allow them to move to head-up or inside leverage.

Here is our base alignment with our back 8.

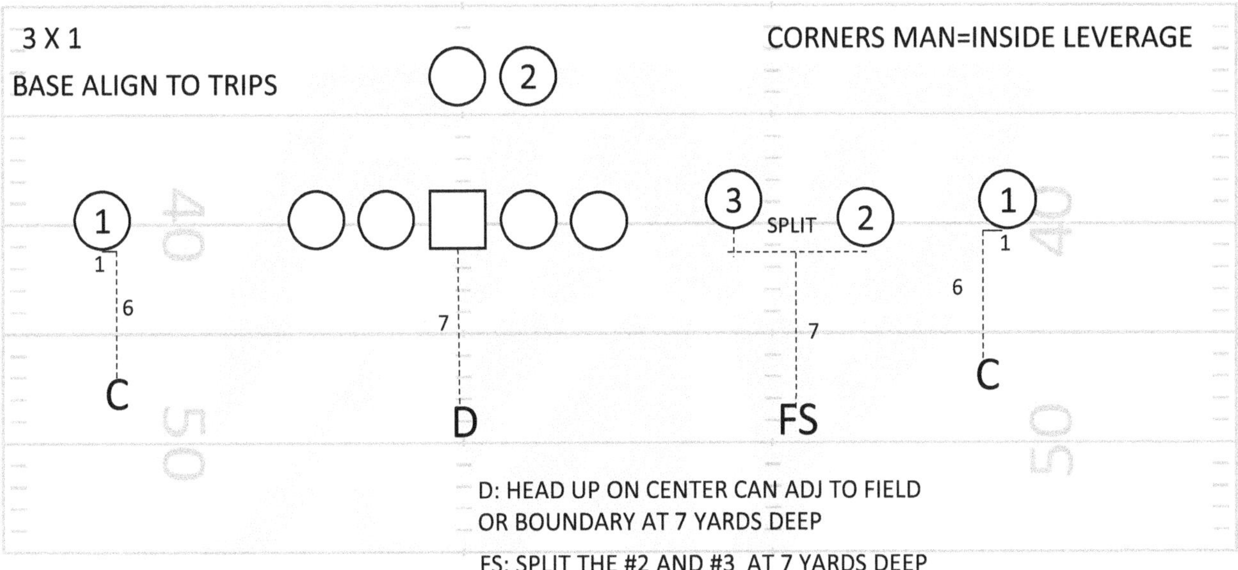

Base alignment to trips.

SAFETY COVERAGE RULES

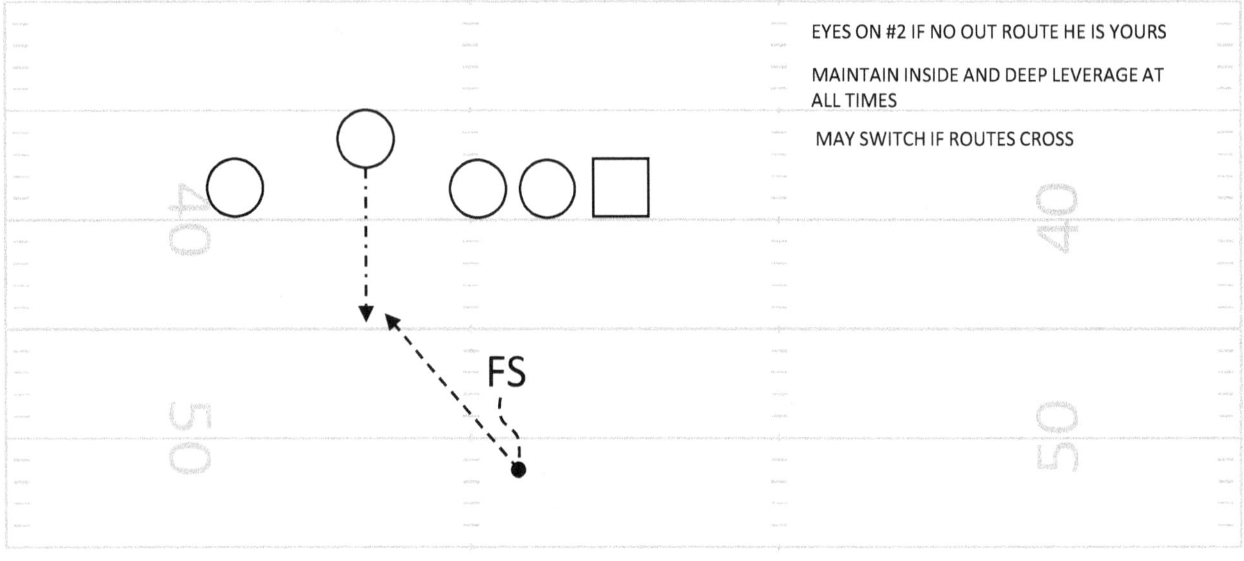

CURL FLAT

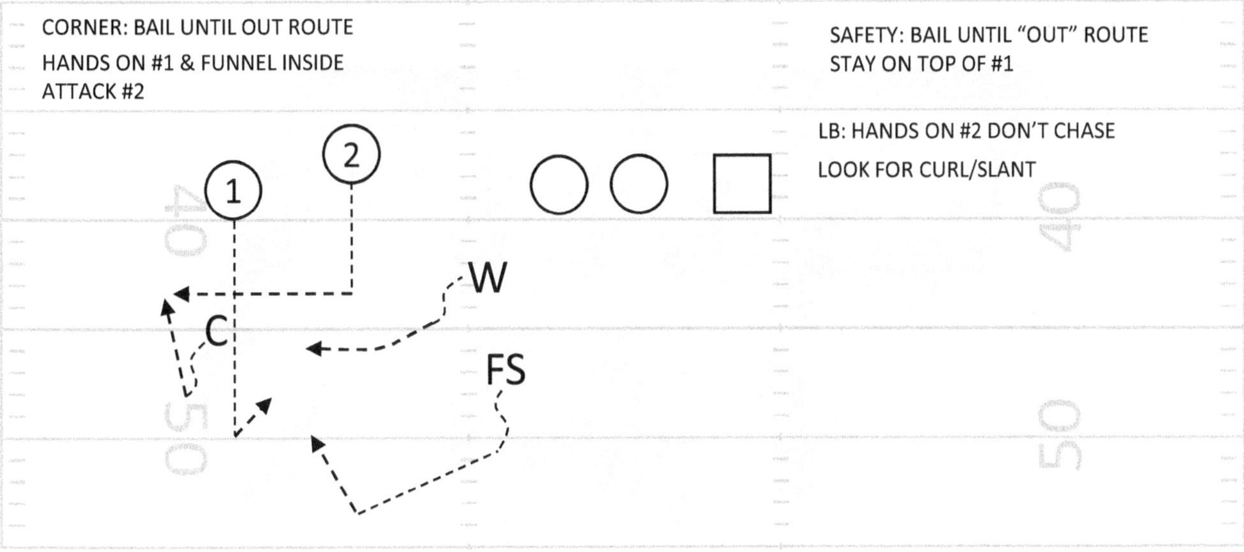

Base route combinations are shown on the next few pages. Here is how we would teach coverage.

On the curl-flat – our corner would work through the outside of the curl as he recognizes the out route. Our Safety would stay inside leverage to make sure there is no deep route coming and then drive on the curl. Our OLB would release the out as he jumps under the curl.

BENCH

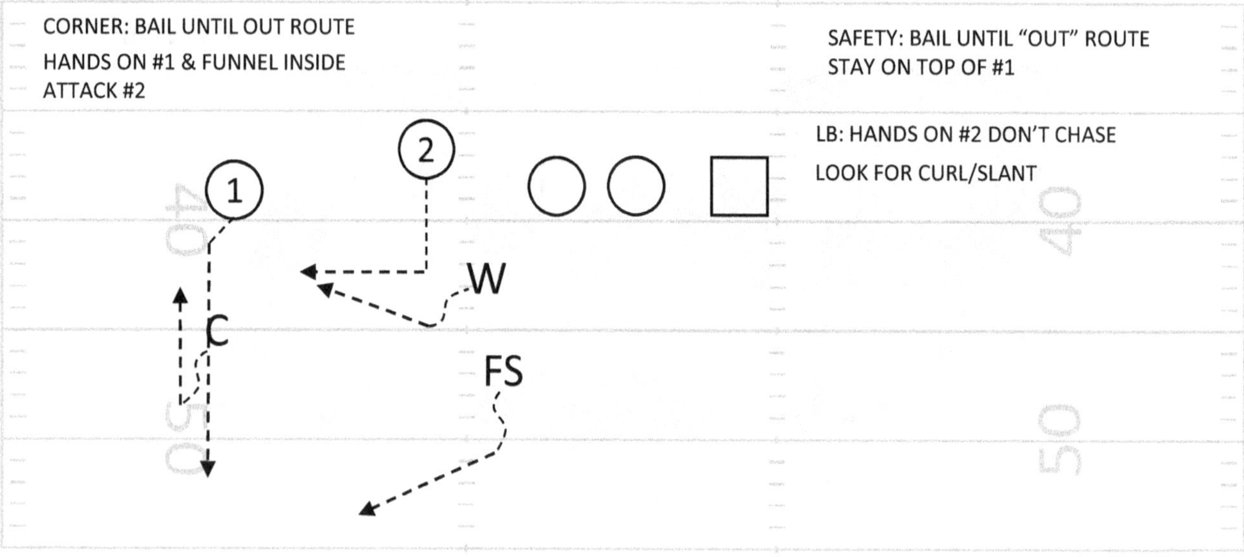

On a "Bench" route –

Corner would run through outside shoulder of #1 to the flats as he reads the out route.

Safety would work over the top of #1 on the go route.

OLB would check for curl and be late to the flats.

SMASH

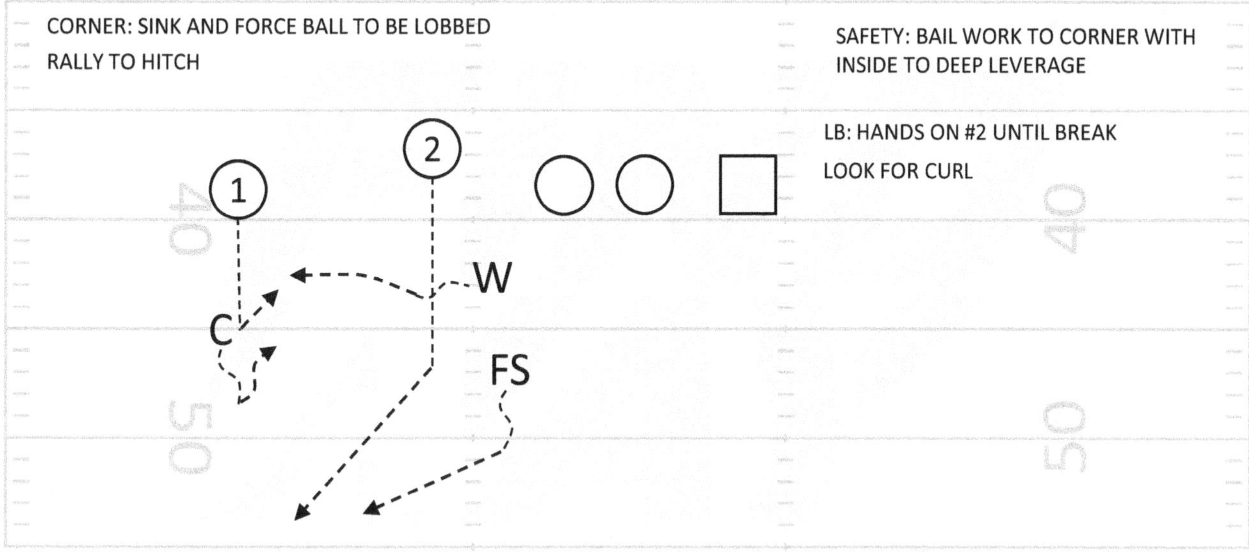

On a "Smash" route –

Corner would bail until he recognized the hitch and drive on the route.

Safety would work over the top of #2 on the corner route.

OLB would disrupt the corner on way to the flats.

"SWITCH"

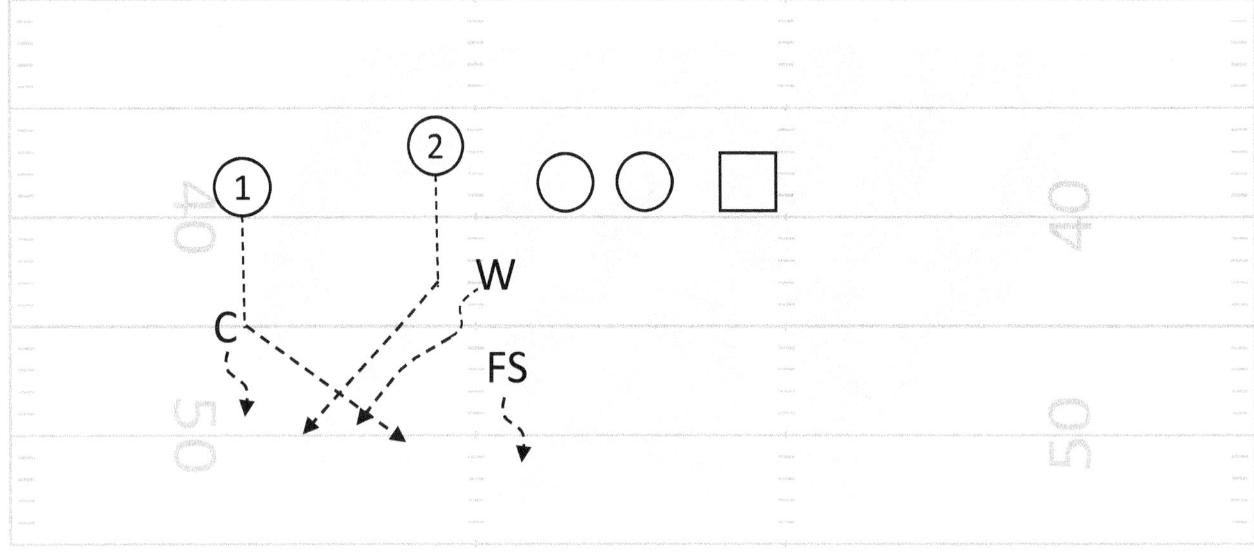

One of the drills we work often is a "switch concept". This is the diagram and rules are below.

Position	Alignment - Assignment
W	HANDS ON #2 LOOK FOR CURL
E	HANDS ON #2 LOOK FOR CURL – (mirrored concepts)
C	SINK AND SWITCH WITH SAFETY
FS	BAIL AND SWITCH WITH THE CORNER
C	SINK AND SWITCH WITH SAFETY

Trips
Coverages and Checks

TRIPS COVERAGE

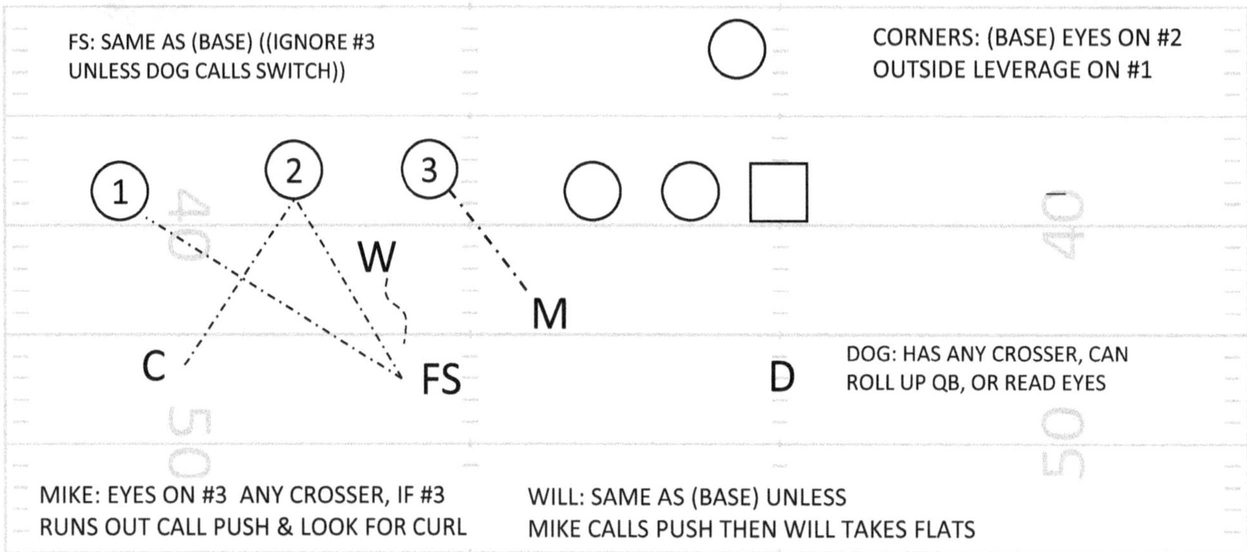

To the trips side in our base coverage we try to keep it as simple as possible.

C/FS/W – All play it the exact same as Twins.

Mike – Will get hands on 3 and eyes on 2-1 for any crossers

Dog – Will poach across for any vertical routes that come down the middle of the field.

Covering a Single

SINGLE BASE NO CALL

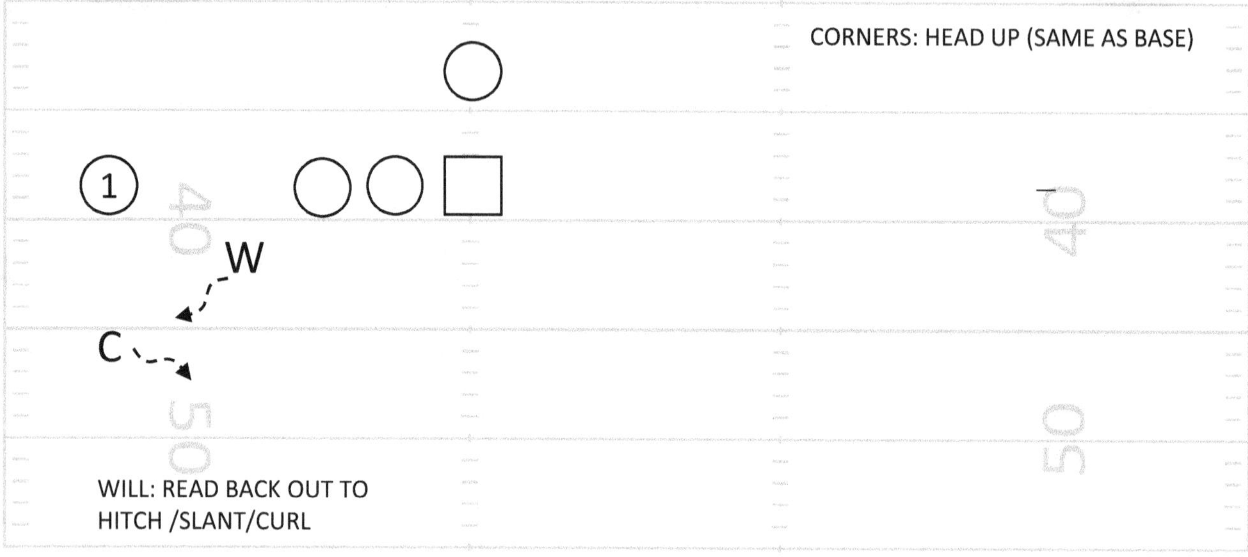

How we handle a single WR depends often on the ability level of the WR, of our corner as well as field position, and scheme of the offense. With all that said here are our base checks to a single WR.

If we make no call, we will give help with our OLB on all slants/curls and react to shorter routes.

SINGLE "HOLD"

CORNERS: OFF AND OUTSIDE LEVERAGE BY (DOWN & DISTANCE, ABILITY)

1

W

C

WILL: "JAM" TAKE AWAY INSIDE ROUTES AT LOS, SINK AND FIND THE BACK

On a "hold" call we will align to Jam the WR. We will often use this against a very talented WR who could create a mismatch.

SINGLE OLB FIRE

CORNERS NO HELP ALIGN INSIDE
“NOW”
(DEPTH DEENDS ON ABILITY)

WILL: STUNT FROM EDGE
MUST PEEL IF BACK FLARES

A stunt is something we will often look to do if we feel we can match up with the WR or are looking to bring pressure quickly.

Roll Coverage

ROLL

One of our first coverage adjustments is our "roll" coverage. We want this to be a quick adjustment to get numbers to a problem area. Our goal is that this looks the same to an offense pre-snap, but attacks after the ball has been snapped.

The next few pages will go through a few scenarios and rules. We call this by the position (or even name of the athlete) to make it easy to understand. We are basically taking the thinking and pattern read out of the equation if we call this coverage.

However, by doing it this way we can get to a roll cover 3 look or even a "trap" cover 2 look with a corner. Our athletes simply know this as "roll".

ROLL RULES

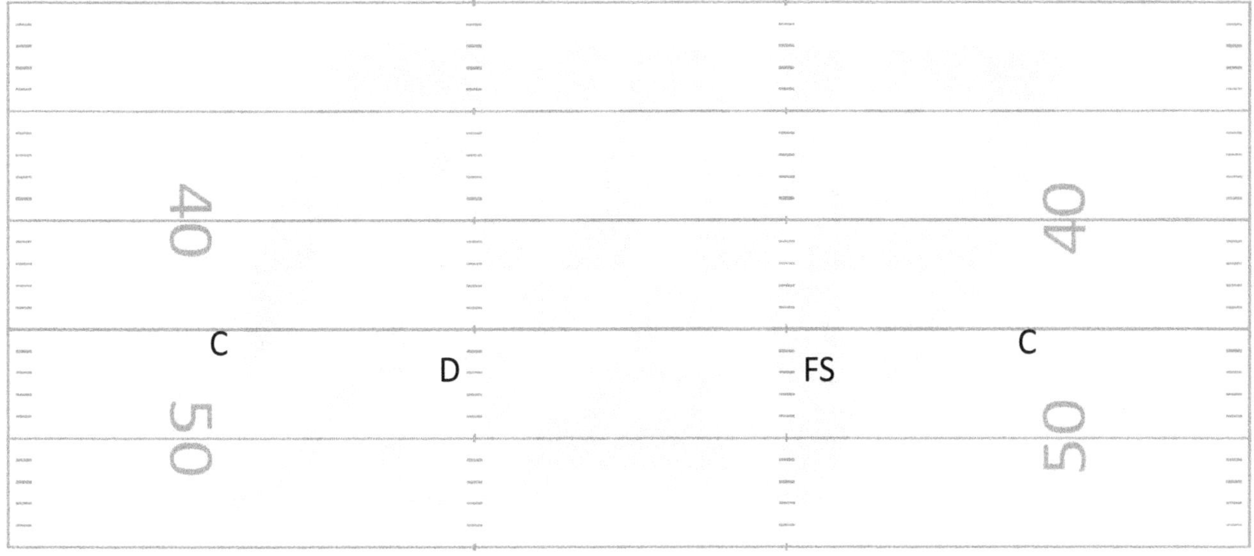

1 FLAT FOOTED AT SNAP MAINTAIN PRE-SNAP DEPTH

2 COLLISION ALL ROUTES IN YOUR AREA

3 WORK TO IF “OUTS” SCREEN/ HITCH

4 IF NOT ROLLING, DROP TO DEEP “THIRDS” STAY DEEP AND KEEP LEVERAGE

CORNER ROLL VS (2X2)

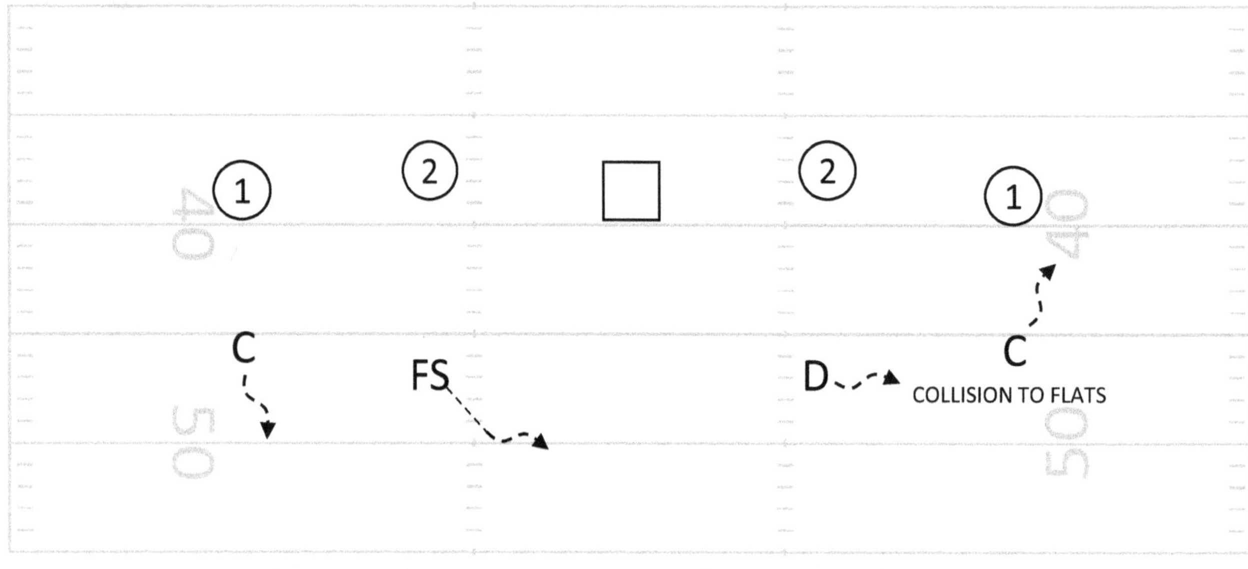

CORNER ROLL VS (2X2)

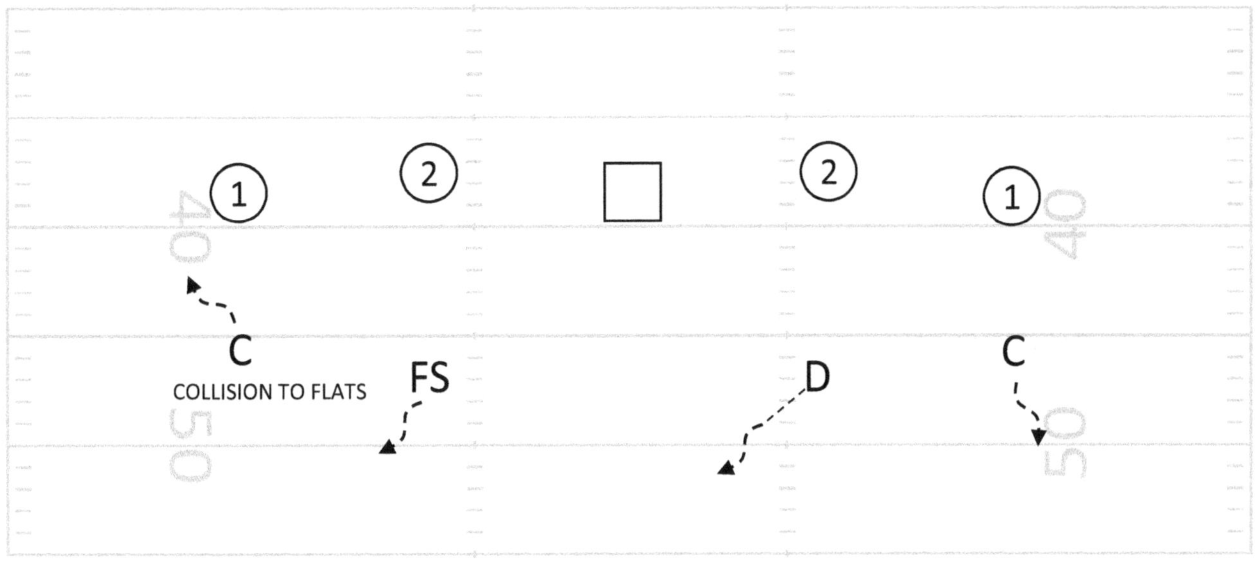

CORNER ROLL VS (3X1)

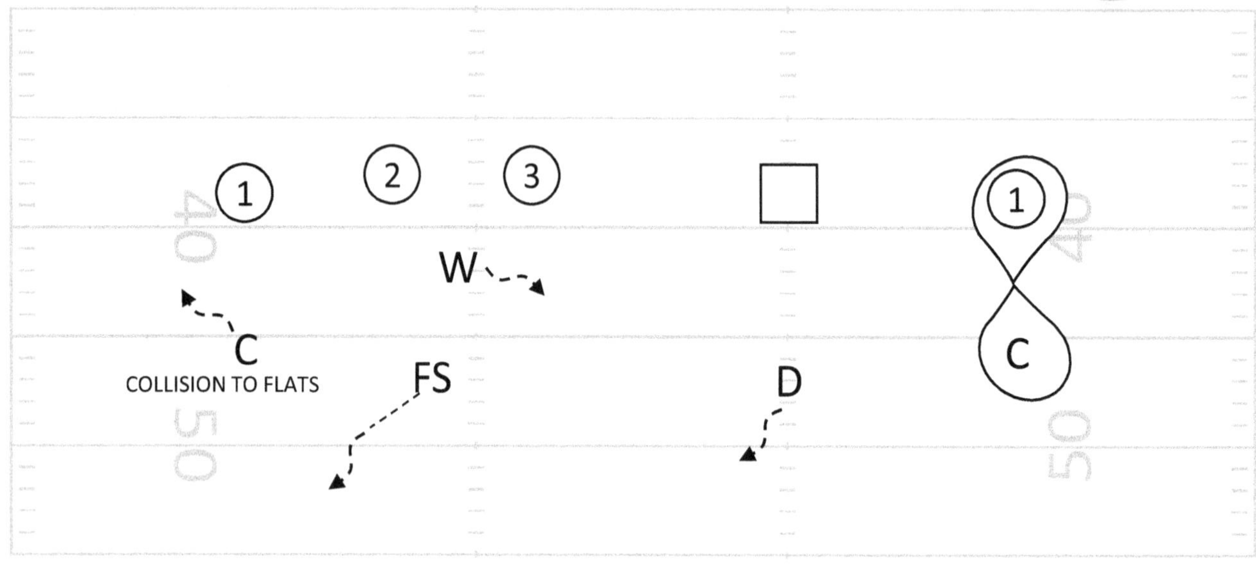

FREE ROLL VS (2X2)

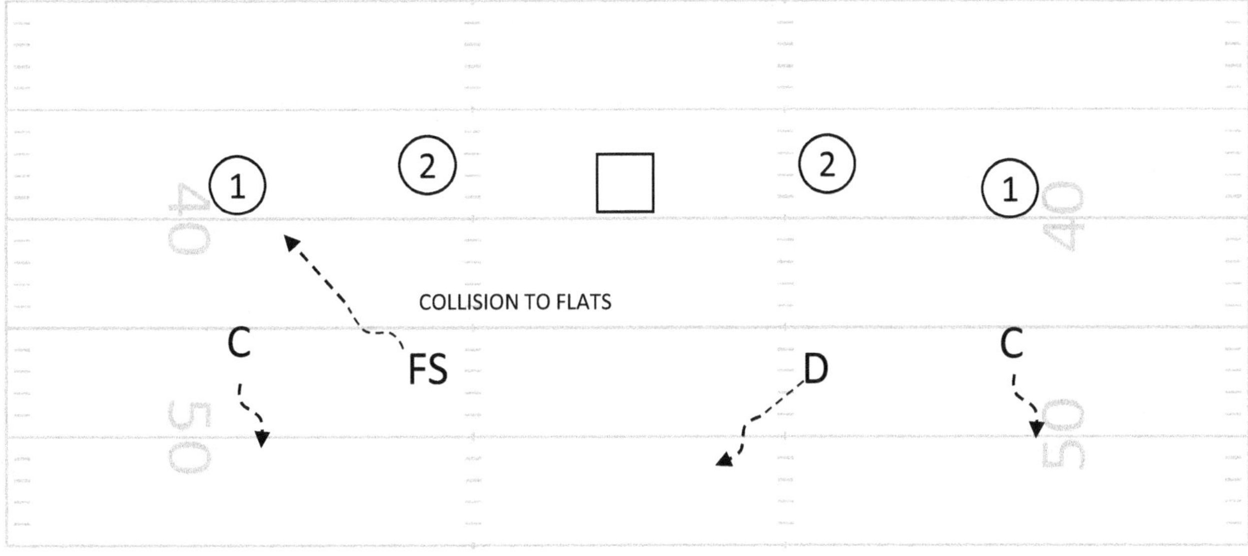

FREE ROLL VS (3X1)

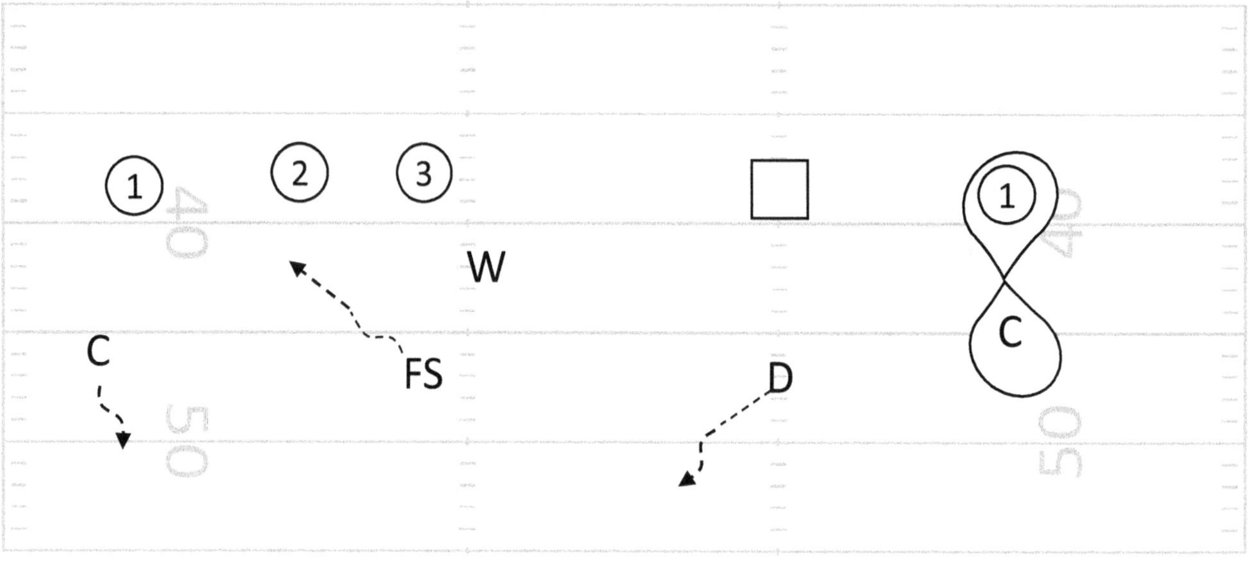

DOG ROLL VS (2X2)

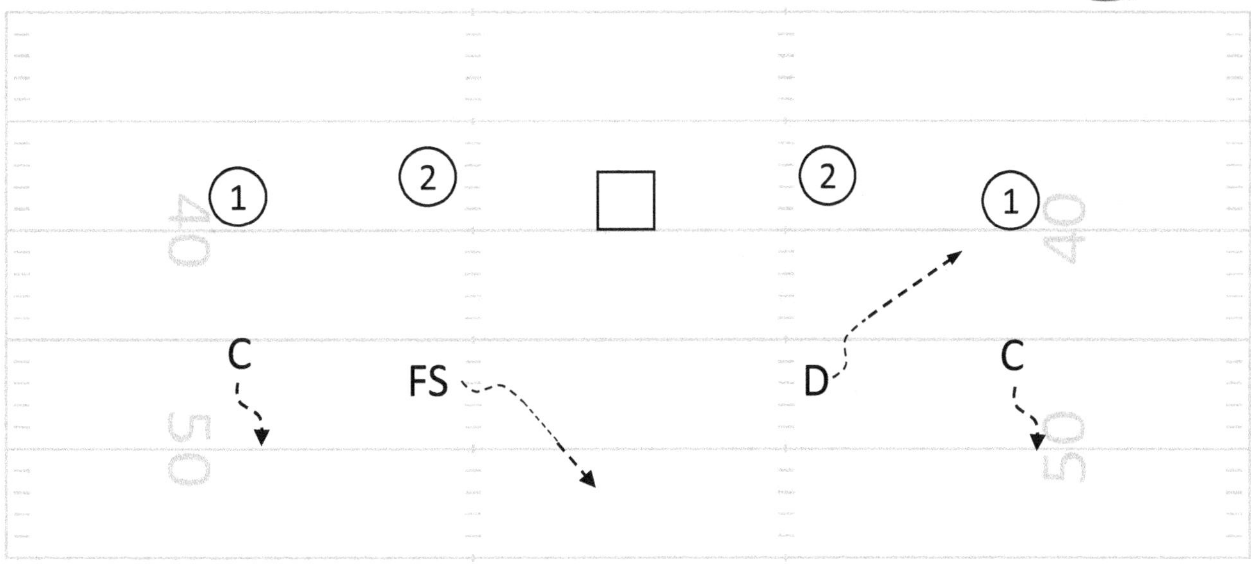

DOG ROLL VS (3X1)

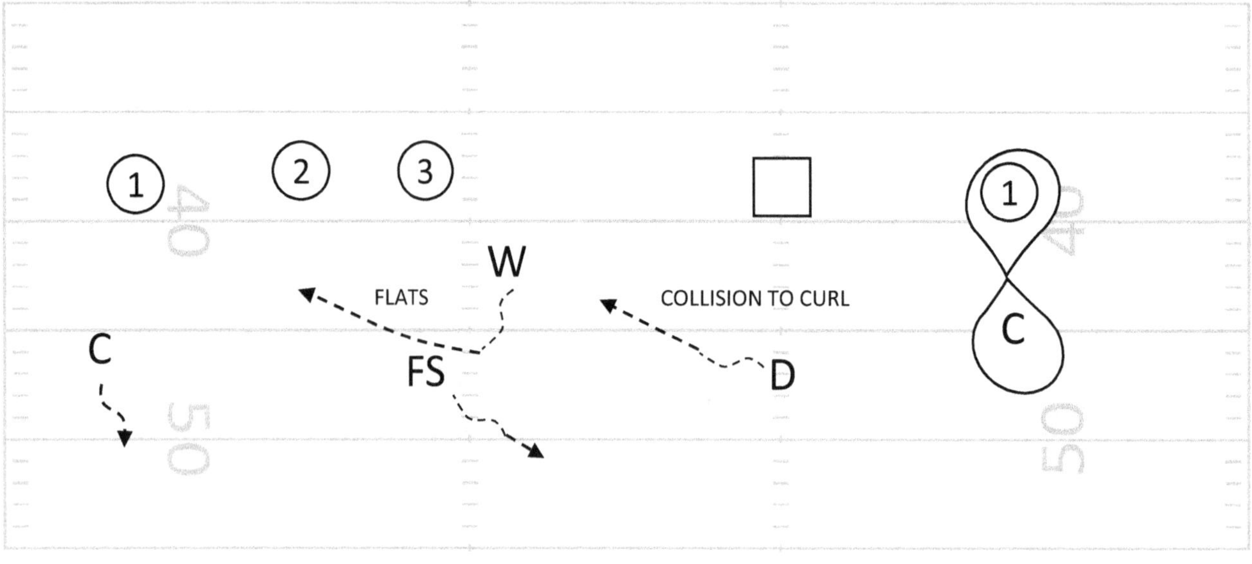

CORNER ROLL VS. (3X1)

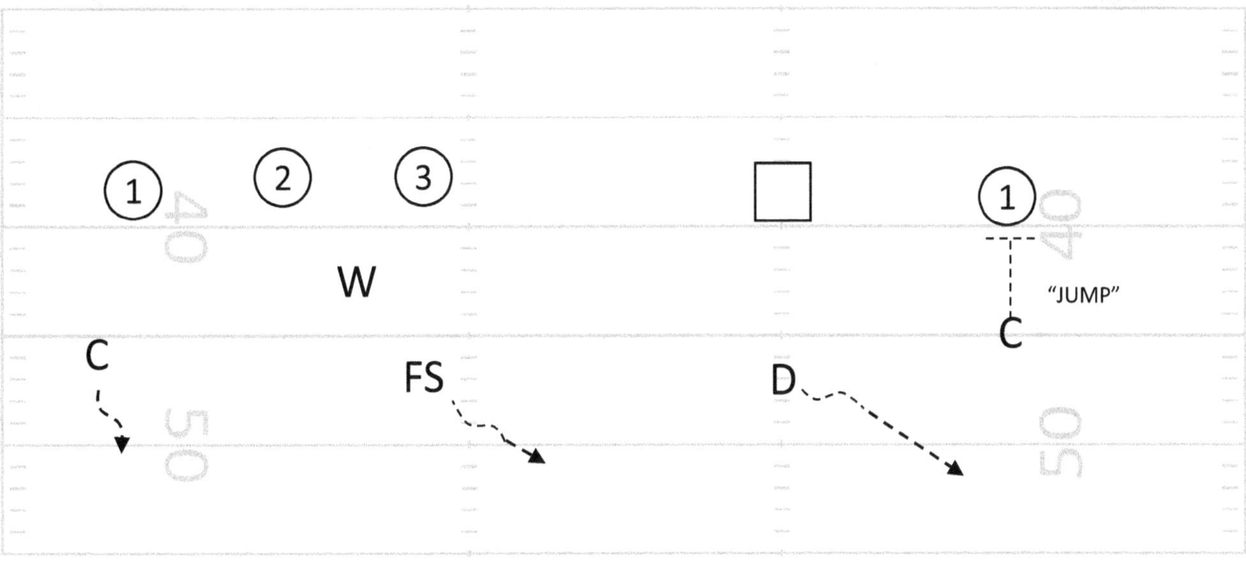

FIND
WAY

KENNY SIMPSON'S
FIT & SWARM
34 DEFENSE
A VERSATILE HIGH SCHOOL SYSTEM

Blitzes

BLITZES

We want a simple system that can send our LB's or DB's to attack with a one-word call.

Our key word is "Fire". If a player hears this with their position, they blitz into their run gap they are responsible for.

If we want to bring them to another gap, we have the words "twist" for our OLB's to stunt to the inside gap and the DL to move outside.

If we want to bring our ILB's off the edge we simply call "Edge".

In the next pages you will see our calls for each position. We also have "full blitzes" that I will cover later in this book.

END "FIRE"

END "FIRE"

B N A E

40 40

50 50

BLITZES ARE CALLED FIRST "FIRE" IF PLAYER IS STUNTING THROUGH RUN FIT

WILL “FIRE”

WILL “FIRE”

W B N A

40 40 50 50

MIKE "FIRE"

MIKE "FIRE"

B

N

A

M

SAM “FIRE”

SAM “FIRE”

B N A

S

FIND
WAY

WILL "TWIST"

KENNY SIMPSON'S
FIT & SWARM
34 DEFENSE
A VERSATILE HIGH SCHOOL SYSTEM

WILL "TWIST"
B
N
A
W
40
40
50
50
"TWIST" TELLS OLB TO SWITCH GAPS WITH DL

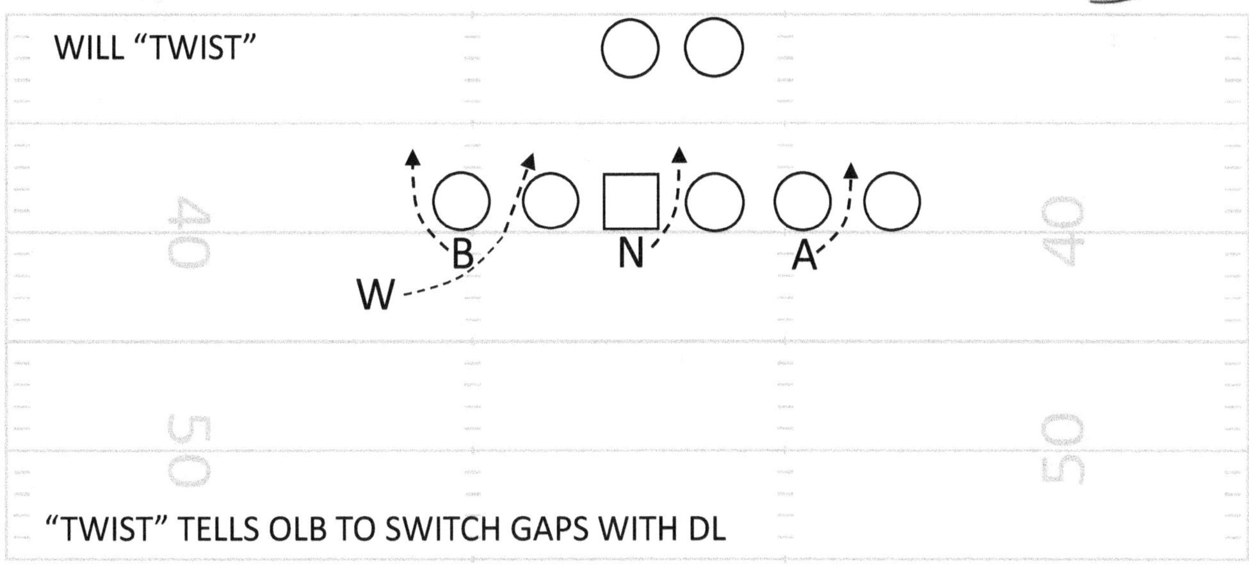

END “TWIST”

END “TWIST”

B N A E

40 40

50 50

MIKE "EDGE"

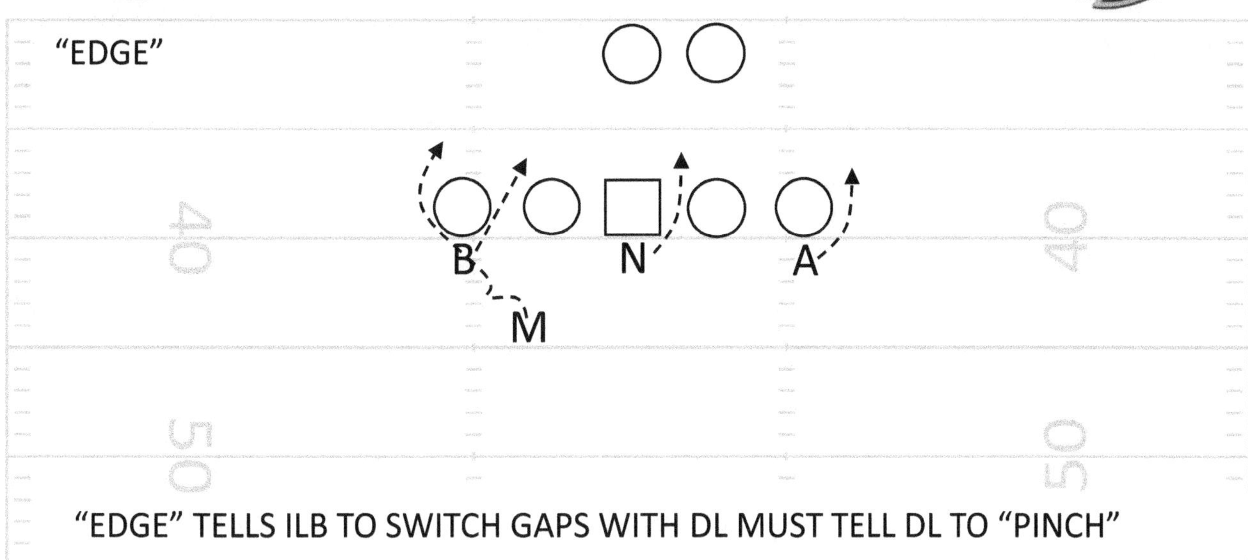

SAM "EDGE"

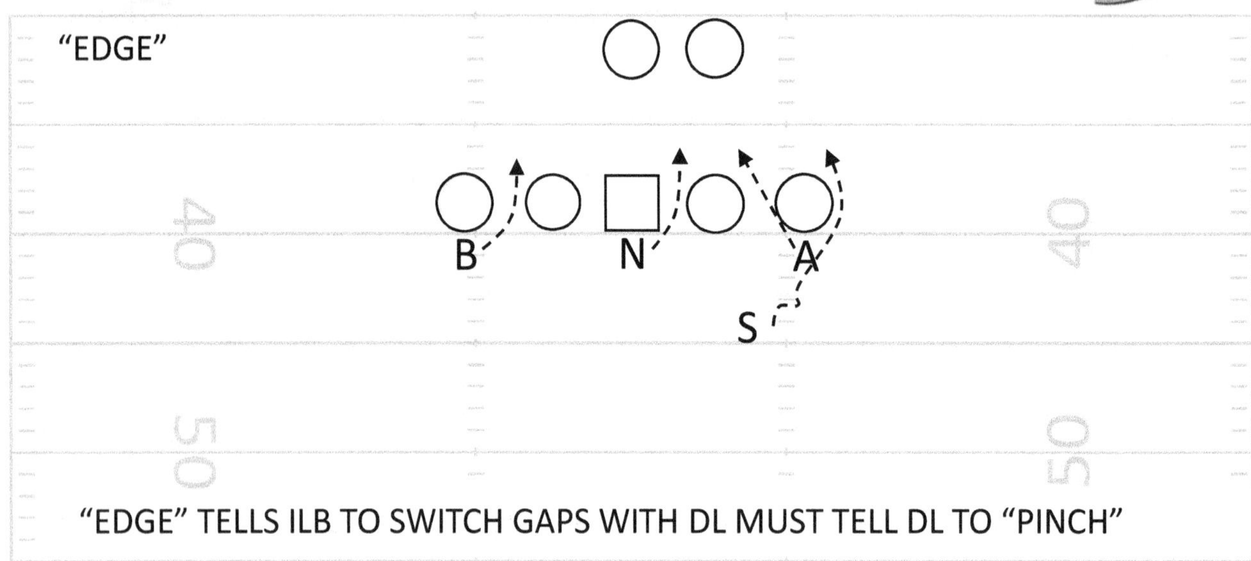

Our blitz combos are one-word tags to bring multiple players. We usually start with 1-2 team blitzes and attempt to make them as multiple as possible with “tags”.

Once we understand the blitz, we simply tag other players to perform the jobs. This makes one “blitz” many looks for an offense.

In the following pages I walk through our “Caveman” and “Tango” blitzes and tags.

FIND WAY

CAVEMAN

KENNY SIMPSON'S
FIT & SWARM
34 DEFENSE
A VERSATILE HIGH SCHOOL SYSTEM

A: PINCH
B: PINCH
N: CAN 2 GAP PICK
A SIDE RIP/LIZ
B
N
A
E
W
M
S
M/S WIDEN TO "40"
WILL: STUNT FROM EDGE

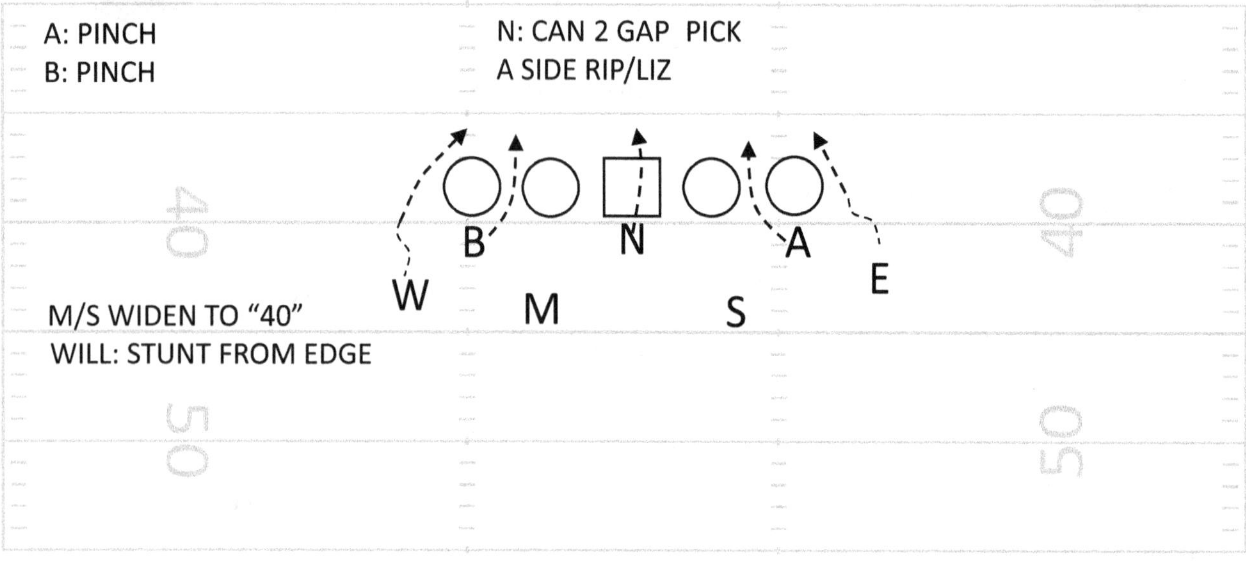

CAVEMAN MIKE X

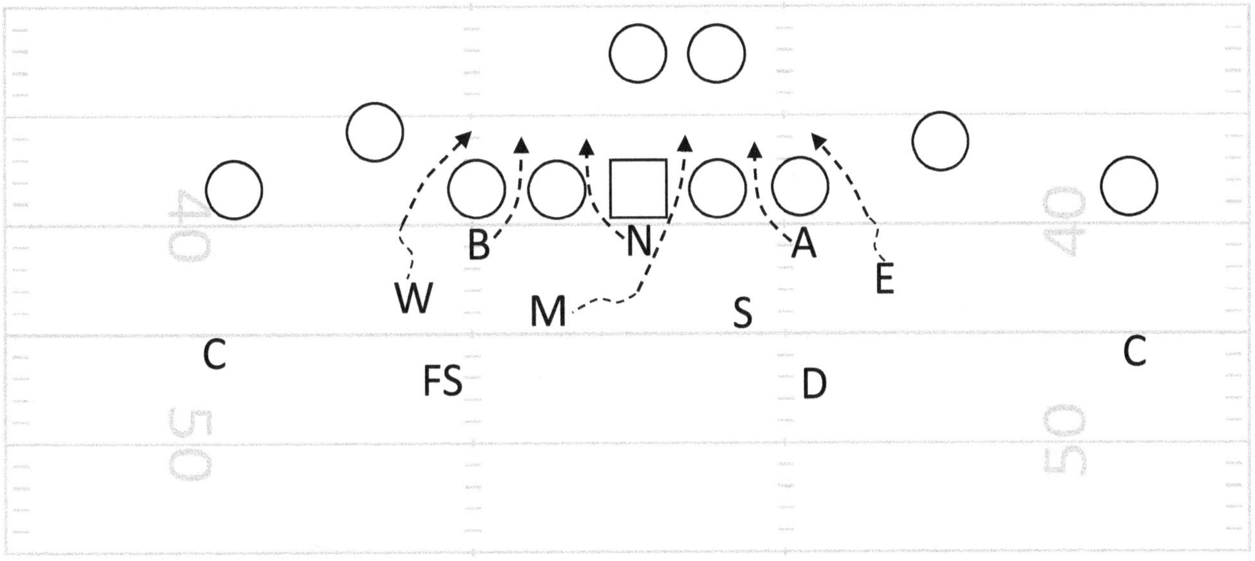

This is the same blitz, but we are “tagging” our Mike to fire also.

TANGO

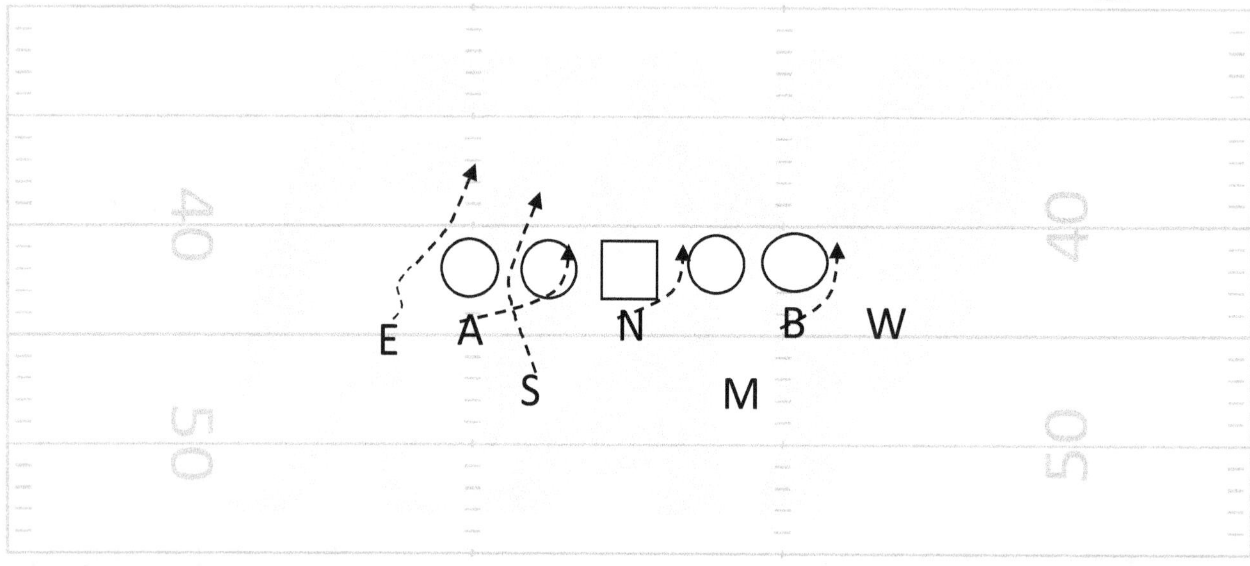

Position	WEAK "TANGO"
A	TWO GAPS THROUGH THE GUARDS HEADGEAR
N	RIP / LIZ STRONG SIDE A GAP
B	RIP / LIZ SRTONG SIDE C GAP
S	CREEP AND STUNT B GAP
E	STUNT FROM EDGE

TANGO DOG

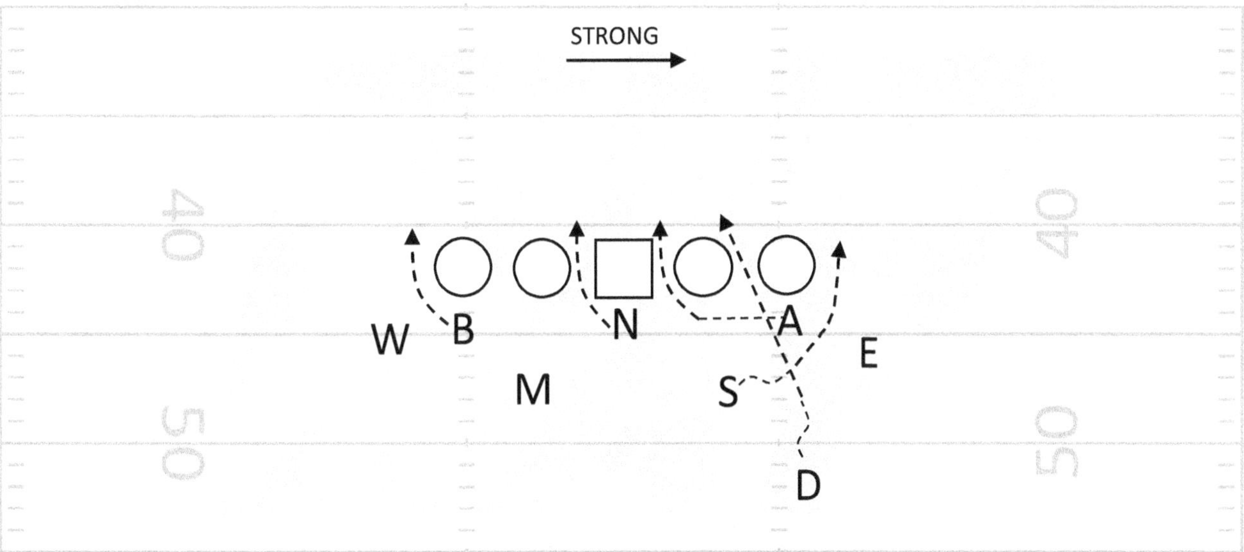

Position	"TANGO" DOG * MUST RUN ROLL COVEAGE*
A	TWO GAPS THROUGH THE GUARDS HEADGEAR
N	RIP / LIZ STRONG SIDE "A" GAP
B	RIP / LIZ SRTONG SIDE "C" GAP
S	CREEP AND STUNT "C" GAP
D	CREEP AND STUNT "B" GAP

WEAK TANGO

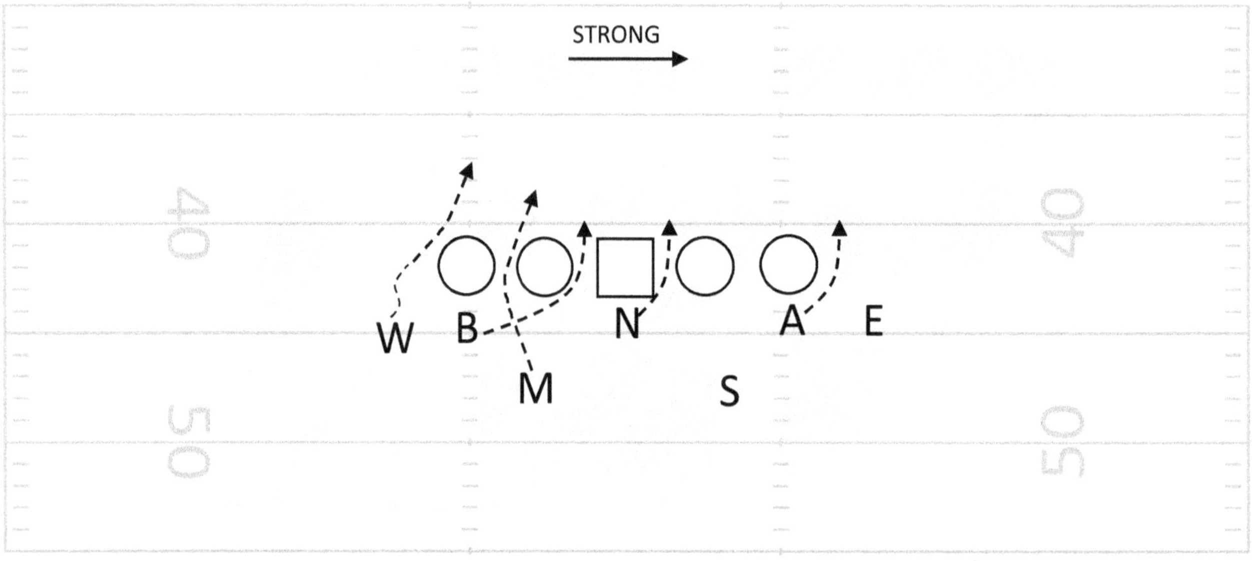

Position	WEAK "TANGO"
B	TWO GAPS THROUGH THE GUARDS HEADGEAR
N	RIP / LIZ STRONG SIDE A GAP
A	RIP / LIZ SRTONG SIDE C GAP
M	CREEP AND STUNT B GAP
W	STUNT FROM EDGE

Blitzes with Coverage

SLANT- MIKE FIRE

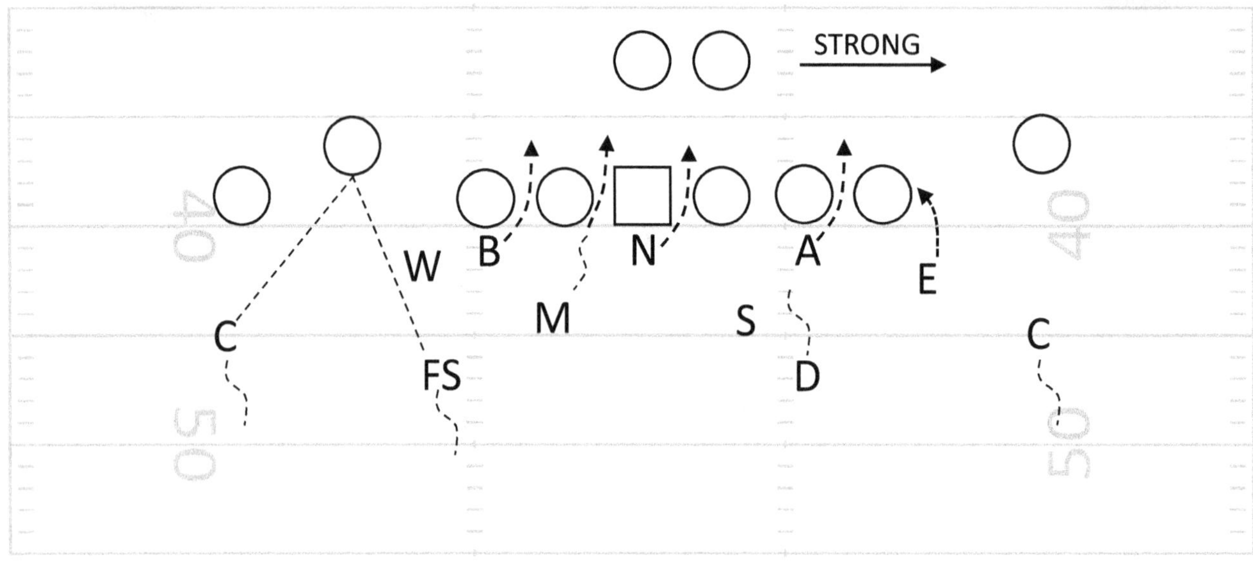

RIP - WILL TWIST

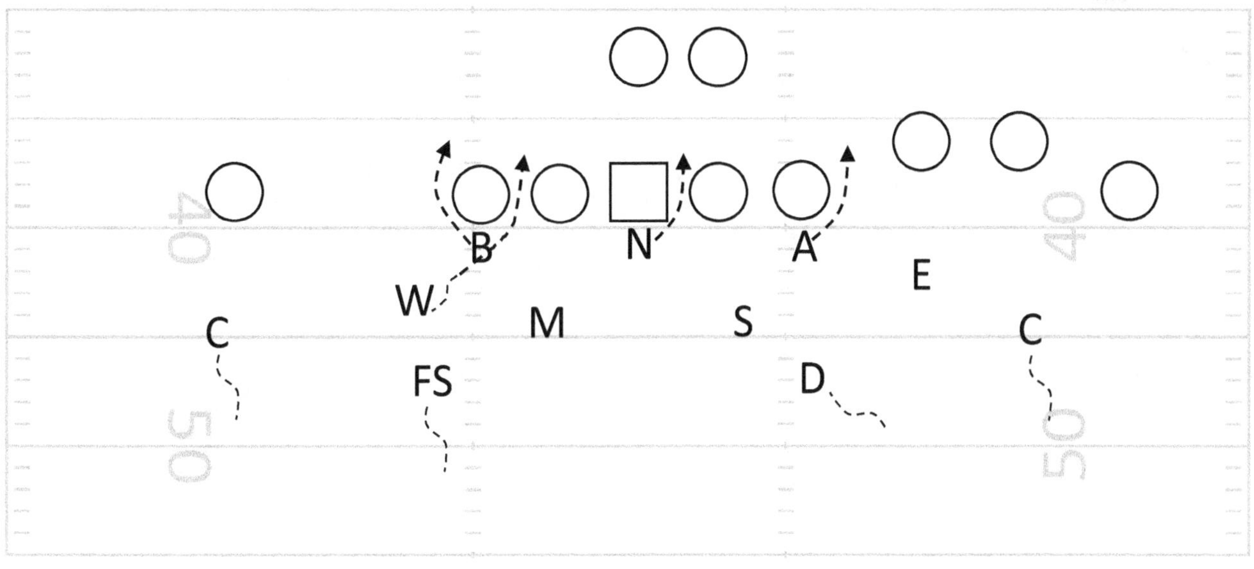

PINCH - END FIRE FREE ROLL

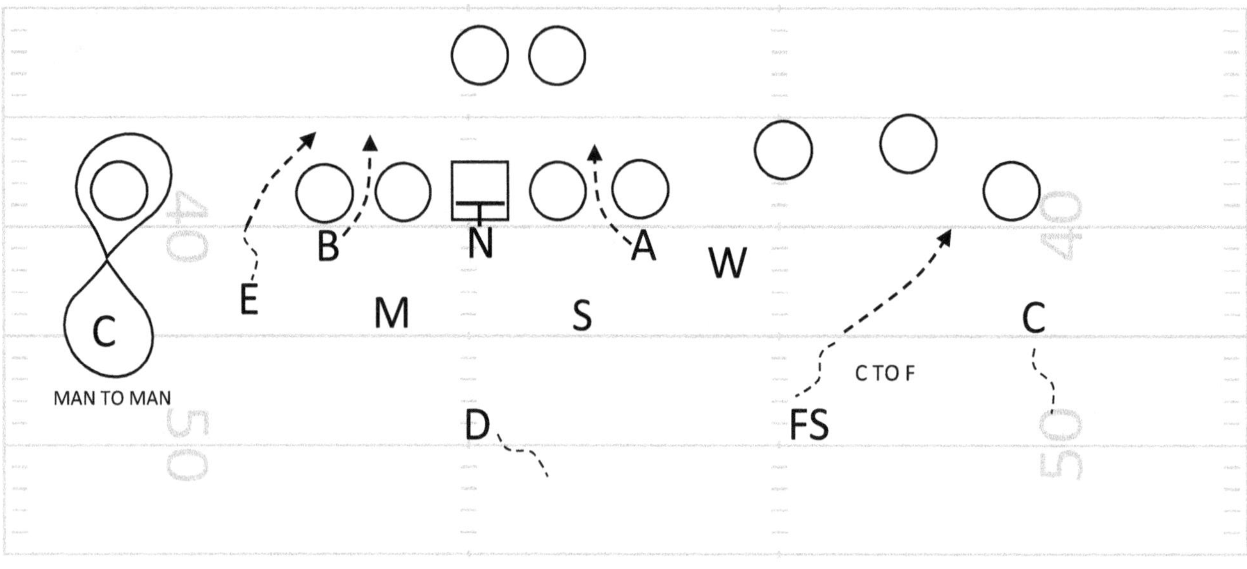

MIKE FIRE CORNER ROLL

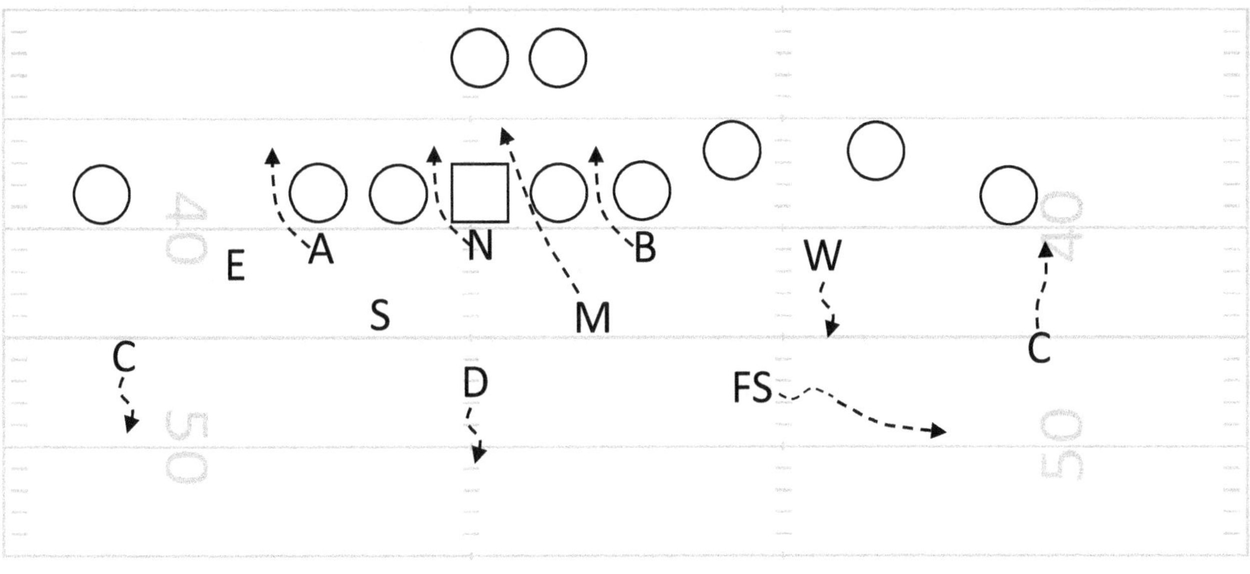

WEAK TANGO FREE ROLL

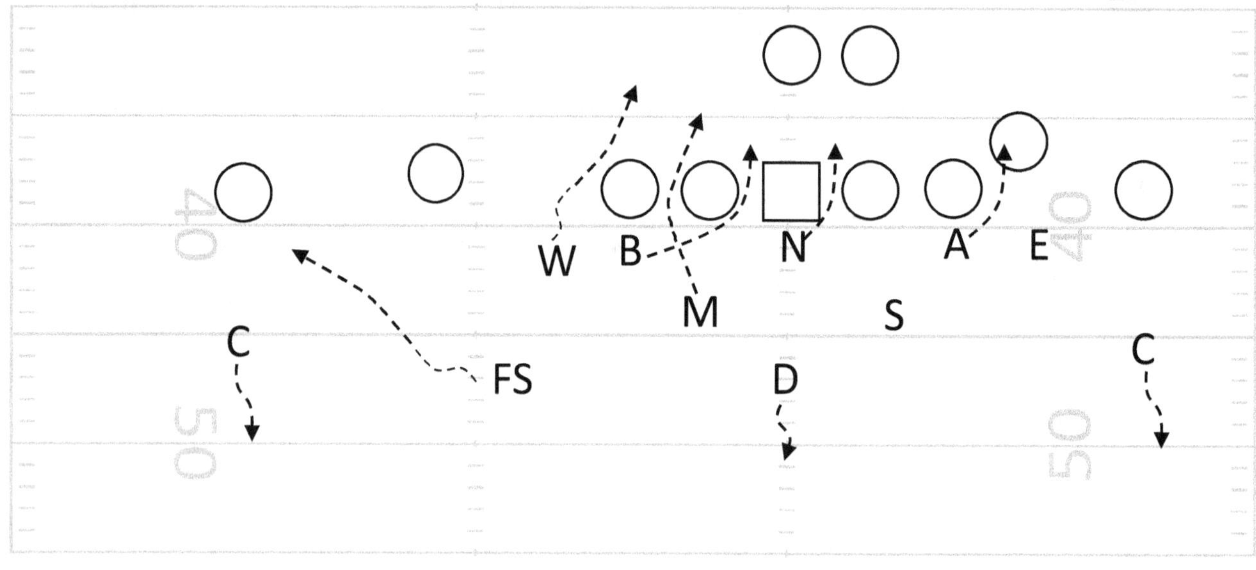

CONCLUSION

CONCLUSION

I want to thank you for your support of my materials. This defense has served me well for many years, but like any defense it needs to continue to grow and evolve. So, use this book as a guide and please reach out to let me know how it is going at your school if you choose to install it.

The coaching community is a great community to be a small part of and I am beyond surprised with the response I have received.

For those of you interested:
The entire system can be found on Coachtube.com:

There is also more information on my website:

Feel free to also reach out with questions:
FBCoachSimpson@gmail.com

Coach Simpson
FindAWay

Coach Simpson is currently the Head Football Coach at Searcy High School, a 6A school in Arkansas. Before taking the job at Searcy, Simpson was the Head Football Coach at Southside High School, a 4A school in Arkansas. Taking over a program that had won eight games in five seasons and had been on a 20+ game losing streak, Simpson led Southside to the playoffs for four-consecutive seasons and won two conference titles. For his efforts, he was named 4A-2 Conference Coach of the Year (2017), named to the as a finalist for Hooten's Coach of the Year (2017) and has been the All-Star Nominee for the 4A-2 (2016 and 2019).

This is Coach Simpson's 7th book. He was a best-selling author for his first work Find a Way: What I Wish I'd Known When I Became a Head Football Coach. The book was released in 2019 and is available on FBCoachSimpson.com. It has sold over 2300 copies as of 2020. This is also the 2.0 version of the GUN-T-RPO offense. The first book has already sold over 1000 copies in just 6 short months.

This is his first book in a series that will feature the 34 Defense. Look for more books later this year.

Simpson raised over $1.5 million for Southside during his 9 seasons and oversaw several major facility projects including: New Field Turf, Expansion to Fieldhouse, Expansion to the school's home bleachers, and the addition of a press box and a new video-board.

Prior to Southside, Simpson took over as Head Coach at Alabama Christian Academy in Montgomery, Alabama. During his tenure there, Simpson took over a team that had been 4-18 and led them to their first home playoff game in over 20-years. For his efforts he was named Montgomery Advertiser's All-Metro Coach of the Year as well as being voted 4A Region 2 Coach of the Year (2010). Simpson also served as the head track coach at ACA and led the girl's and boy's teams to multiple top 10 finishes in 4A.

Simpson began his coaching career at Madison Academy, in Huntsville, Alabama. He served as a junior high basketball and football coach, before working into a varsity coaching role in football. He graduated from Harding University in 2003. He is married to Jamey and has three children: Avery, Braden and Bennett. The couple was married in 2001 after meeting at Harding University.

Contact Coach Simpson

@FBCoachSimpson – Twitter
Kenny Simpson – Facebook
FBCoachSimpson.com

www.ingramcontent.com/pod-product-compliance
Lightning Source LLC
LaVergne TN
LVHW061247100826
845148LV00008B/1053
9781735159140